EMPLOYED FOR LIFE

This book is part of the Peter Lang Education list.
Every volume is peer reviewed and meets
the highest quality standards for content and production.

PETER LANG
New York • Washington, D.C./Baltimore • Bern
Frankfurt • Berlin • Brussels • Vienna • Oxford

DR. TRACEY WILEN
AND DR. COURTNEY L. VIEN
WITH GARY DAUGENTI

Employed for Life
21ST-CENTURY CAREER TRENDS

PETER LANG
New York • Washington, D.C./Baltimore • Bern
Frankfurt • Berlin • Brussels • Vienna • Oxford

Library of Congress Cataloging-in-Publication Data

Wilen, Tracey.
Employed for life: 21st-century career trends /
Tracey Wilen, Courtney L. Vien, Gary Daugenti.
pages cm
Includes bibliographical references.
1. Career development. 2. Personnel management. 3. Technological innovations.
4. Employees—Effect of technological innovations on. 5. Vocational qualifications.
I. Vien, Courtney L. II. Daugenti, Gary. III. Title.
HF5381.W5485   650.14—dc23   2013042278
ISBN 978-1-4331-2544-7 (hardcover)
ISBN 978-1-4331-2543-0 (paperback)
ISBN 978-1-4539-1259-1 (e-book)

Bibliographic information published by **Die Deutsche Nationalbibliothek**.
Die Deutsche Nationalbibliothek lists this publication in the "Deutsche
Nationalbibliografie"; detailed bibliographic data is available
on the Internet at http://dnb.d-nb.de/.

The paper in this book meets the guidelines for permanence and durability
of the Committee on Production Guidelines for Book Longevity
of the Council of Library Resources.

© 2014 Peter Lang Publishing, Inc., New York
29 Broadway, 18th floor, New York, NY 10006
www.peterlang.com

Printed in the United States of America

CONTENTS

ACKNOWLEDGMENTS

The authors would like to thank the following individuals for their contributions to this book:

HR professionals:
Allison Allen, Rich Andersen, Andrew Greenberg, Pamela Hardy, Rich James, Sara Lautenbach, Katherine Markgraf, Keith Meyerson, Meg Paradise, Megan Remark, Karen Robinson, Christine Roggenbusch, Tim Russell, Nancy Sullivan, Sam Wageman

Recruiting professionals:
Rich Andersen, Anne Angelopoulos, Jennifer Brent, Lisa Francone, Leslie Lazarus, Sheila Maultsby, Elsa Meyer, Kyle Misiak, Maureen Perkins, Carolyn Redman, Rich Smith, Jim Stroud, Sam Wageman

Contributors of surveys and research studies:
Gent & Associates, Juststaff

Graphics:
Linda Fisher

Times Have Changed— Has Your Career Plan?

Not that long ago, careers in the corporate world were fairly straightforward. You'd earn a college degree and go to work for a company where the vast majority of your colleagues would be white and male. The company would train and develop you. You'd move up the ladder, gaining power, prestige, and income along the way. Even if you didn't work for the same firm for your entire career, you'd probably stay within the same industry. You'd retire at around 65, perhaps collecting a generous pension and the proverbial gold watch, or perhaps not, but certainly planning to live off your ample savings.

Those days are long gone. Now, workers spend an average of only four years at a job and often have more than one career during their lifetimes. Most careers aren't linear upward climbs any more; instead, they resemble lattices or labyrinths, as employees have greater freedom to change industries, freelance, take sabbaticals, return to school, opt for part-time work, or pursue business ownership as their life circumstances change. Companies engage in less training and a single college degree will no longer carry a worker throughout her career. The workforce is considerably more diverse in terms of race, gender, and national background. Pensions are a thing of the past, and retiring at 65 is no longer a viable option for many people.

But many workers behave as though the old paradigm is still in place. They assume they'll stay with one company until they retire or are forced out, and believe that their education ended with their bachelor's degree. They don't keep up with trends in their industry and are caught off guard when they're laid off or their company goes out of business. They believe that being good enough at a static set of skills will ensure their employability, and are surprised when they aren't hired or when more agile workers are promoted over them. They see working for a large corporation as their only employment option, and anticipate their career will end when they retire in their mid-60s.

This mindset is long out of date, and can be a barrier to employability in today's career marketplace. If it sounds like yours, even a little bit, we suggest changing the way you think about your working life. View yourself not as a worker bee who'll be rewarded for diligence and talent but as an entrepreneur: someone who sets a clear strategy for his or her career, but isn't afraid to make changes when things aren't going as planned; who understands and markets his or her strengths; who takes calculated risks; who researches his or her "customers"—potential employers—and gives them what they want; and who's always innovating.

In this book, we'll share some ways you can move towards this entrepreneurial mindset. In Chapters 1, 2, and 3, we'll show you the cultural and technological factors that are changing work forever, what that means for your career, and which skills and characteristics you need to cultivate to be successful in the world of do-it-yourself career planning. Chapter 1 discusses the impact of four societal factors on work: technology; globalization; longevity (and its corollary, members of multiple generations sharing the workplace); and demographics, including the rise of women, the increased ethnic diversity of the United States, and changes in gender roles and family patterns. Chapter 2 describes the shift from linear to labyrinthine careers, one marked by multiple changes in industry and employment type over the course of a working lifetime. It covers such topics as the new values that are driving people's careers; different work patterns within large corporations; and some of the many employment options individuals can choose from, including freelancing, entrepreneurship, and working for small or medium-sized companies. Chapter 3 explores some of today's most prominent technologies, such as big data, social media, cloud computing, and solar power and discusses how they're changing careers by creating new jobs, destabilizing industries, and increasing skill requirements.

In Chapters 4, 5, and 6, we'll share insights from human resources (HR) professionals and recruiters on planning your career, finding jobs, and staying employed. Chapter 4 draws upon interviews with HR professionals to inform you about the latest trends in career development and best career development practices for both individuals and companies. Chapter 5 brings together interviews with recruiters and the results of a survey of successful job seekers to give you insider advice on how to find a job in an employer's market. Chapter 6, written by co-author Gary Daugenti, founder and president of recruiting firm Gent & Associates, is a primer on working with recruiters: the people who have a pipeline to some of the best compensated and most interesting jobs. Daugenti explains how recruiters operate, how to contact them, what to do if they approach you, and some things *not* to do when working with them.

In Chapter 7, we provide you with a simple but powerful framework you can use to plan a career that may last 50 years or longer. This framework will help you visualize the connections between work, education, finances, health, leisure, and your relationship with friends and family, and to foresee a life where all these different strands are brought into balance.

CHAPTER ONE

Societal Forces

How Technology, Globalization, Longevity, and Demographics Will Impact Your Career

Four forces have converged that have changed the workplace forever: the astonishing ascendency of communications technology, particularly the Internet; globalization, which has increased competition but also opportunity for both companies and individual workers; demographic shifts, including increased ethnic diversity, the growing presence of women in the workplace, and a rise in the number of nontraditional families; and extended longevity, which has reshaped the concept of retirement and made it possible to have more than one full-scale career in a lifetime. In this chapter, we look at each of these forces in depth, illustrating how they've changed the workplace and what new skills and characteristics you'll need to acquire as a result.

Technology

If you've ever used your smartphone in a store to check if the price of an item was cheaper online, you've participated in the practice known as *showrooming*. You're not alone: Some 70% of customers say they've researched merchandise on the Internet while shopping offline.[1] Showrooming has proven a blow to brick-and-mortar retailers, who spend vast amounts of money stocking and displaying items only to lose sales to Amazon. The practice has been considered a factor in the demise of such companies as Circuit City, Borders, CompUSA, and Tweeter.[2]

Savvy retailers, however, have adapted to showrooming by changing their business practices. Nordstrom, Target, and Best Buy, for example, compete with online retailers by using such tactics as price matching online competitors, offering superior customer service, improving the shopping experience, implementing reward programs that encourage customers to buy in-store, and introducing mobile payments.[3]

In like fashion, workers need to learn to adjust to new technologies, or risk being left unemployable. Technology has made the employment landscape volatile, as innovations have the potential to disrupt or even eliminate entire industries. (We'll discuss a few of these game-changing innovations in Chapter 3.) Consider, as a cautionary tale, the freestanding GPS device. Just a few short years ago, these gadgets were considered state-of-the-art. Now, sophisticated navigation apps may render them obsolete.[4]

Technology advances with breathtaking speed. To reach 50 million households, it took radio 38 years, television 13 years, the Internet four years, and Facebook just two years.[5] In 2005, just 8% of Americans used social networks; in 2011, 65% did.[6] eBay was only launched in 1995, Google in 1998, Facebook in 2004, Twitter in 2006, and Instagram in 2010, and yet it's hard to imagine life without them.

Thus, to stay employable today, you must not expect that your company and industry will remain static for long. Think of the household-name companies that have gone out of business in recent years because they were unable to adapt to the changes technology brought about. Blockbuster could not compete with Netflix, Borders with Amazon, or Tower Records with iTunes. Kodak invented digital photography but could not capitalize on it. Even that venerable institution, the newspaper, is losing ground to the Internet. Two hundred and twenty newspapers closed between 1990 and 2009, the most recent year for which figures are available, largely because of competition from online news.[7] Some futurists predict that the last print newspaper will go out of business by 2040.[8]

At the same time, the Internet has also created jobs, companies, and entire new industries. The number of jobs in the Internet sector grew 634% over the past decade, more than 200 times the rate of the economy as a whole.[9] US software jobs have grown 562% over the past two decades,[10] while cloud computing services will generate nearly 14 million jobs worldwide by 2015.[11] Facebook, founded in 2004, employs 4,900 people; eBay, founded in 1995, employs over 20,000; and Google, founded in 1998, over 53,000.[12] The Internet has also driven massive economic growth. McKinsey estimates that the Internet was responsible for 21% of the GPD growth in mature economies between 2006 and 2011.[13]

Even as new technologies have reduced the need for such employees as bank tellers, travel agents, and tax preparers, they have created new job categories. Jobs like social media strategist, user experience designer, online community manager, search engine optimization specialist, and app designer, for example, didn't exist

10 years ago. An estimated 53,000 people are now employed making applications for Facebook alone.[14]

In such a fluid environment, you'll need to continually keep abreast of changes in your company and sector, staying informed about innovations and upstart competitors with the potential to destabilize your field. Neither you nor your firm can afford to be complacent. You should be prepared to evaluate and upgrade your skills on an ongoing basis. You'll also be considered a more valuable employee if you cultivate your problem-solving skills, think quickly on your feet, and offer creative solutions to the challenges your company faces.

The Information Revolution

If there's one word synonymous with the Internet, it may well be *information*. The Net has exponentially increased the amount, type, and accessibility of information available to us. Now, with a quick Google search, anyone can uncover information once known only by experts or insiders, from what perks a company offers its employees to what a job candidate thinks of a certain political party, from what twelve different retailers charge for the same product to how tasty the steak is at a bistro in a distant city, from detailed instructions on how to program a computer to how much it costs to ship freight from India. Vast amounts of scientific, technical, business, and personal data are now at the fingertips of anyone with a wireless card or an Ethernet cable.

This information revolution cannot help but change the way we work. For one thing, it's shortened the shelf life of knowledge. In 1986, the typical employee could store 75% of the knowledge she needed to perform her job in her head; now, employees can only store 10%, and knowledge workers spend up to one work day per week looking for information.[15]

It's also altered the way we gain and process the information we need to do our jobs. Workers today need to obtain information both from *knowledge stocks*—static bodies of information like books and training manuals—and *knowledge flows*: ever-changing, constantly updated streams of information like wikis, message boards, and social media. Knowledge flows can often be more useful than knowledge stocks because they change in response to new conditions or discoveries, and draw upon the experiences of many people rather than one or a few.[16]

In an age where the Internet acts as our collective repository of information, employees who are skilled at tapping knowledge flows will be in high demand. In fact, *what* you know is becoming less important than your ability to find and make meaning from information. The information revolution also means that you can no longer expect one college degree to serve you for your entire career. While the critical thinking and researching skills you honed while earning your undergraduate degree will still prove valuable, be prepared to become a lifelong learner who gathers knowledge in both formal and informal settings.

Globalization

The world's nations, markets, and technologies are now interconnected to an unprecedented degree, which is having a profound impact on the way we work. Many multinational businesses no longer have home countries: Chinese-owned Lenovo, for example, is headquartered in New York, runs factories in Beijing and Raleigh, North Carolina, and is listed on the Hong Kong stock exchange.[17] Small businesses can now serve international markets almost as easily as they can local companies. Indian, Chinese, and Brazilian firms successfully compete with US and European ones for knowledge work. The Internet has enabled firms to assemble virtual teams of workers from all across the globe, while microwork platforms like oDesk let freelancers bid for projects in hundreds of nations.

Globalization means that you need to put your career in its global context no matter what field you work in. Your competitors for jobs are no longer just people who live in easy driving distance from your city: They're in the United Kingdom, Germany, Brazil, India, China, and Kenya. Your firm, be it large or small, is likewise competing with companies from around the world. You're almost certainly working with or for, or selling to or buying from, people from outside your nation, who may not speak your language and who may possess some very different cultural values.

In such a climate, you need to market yourself effectively and make yourself as irreplaceable as possible to remain employed. You also need to be culturally sensitive and learn the business etiquette, customs, and possibly even languages of the nations you most often work with. And, as globalization is making work infinitely more complex and uncertain, you should cultivate agility, staying abreast of global events, thinking quickly on your feet, and adapting to changing circumstances.

An Interconnected World

Billions of people worldwide now have access to the Internet, and their numbers are growing. By 2025, more than five billion people will own Internet-enabled mobile devices.[18] This connection to a worldwide network of information allows individuals to be global consumers, employees, and businesspeople. A person's physical location and country of origin now have less impact on his working life than ever before: Almost anyone with Internet access can buy and sell products, track shipments, find information about products and companies (often posted by fellow consumers), apply for jobs, pursue learning and training opportunities, and work with virtual team members, regardless of time, place, or nationality.

Microwork platforms like oDesk, Elance, Freelancer.com, GetACoder, Guru, PeoplePerHour, and iFreelance enable independent contractors to perform knowledge work on a pay-for-performance basis for companies worldwide. Such platforms are highly transparent, letting potential employers view individuals' work histories and performance reviews. They are rapidly growing in popularity.

The number of workers on Elance has more than doubled since 2010,[19] and over $500 million worth of work has been performed on the platform.[20] The number of project management hours logged on oDesk has soared from 1,000 in 2009 to about 50,000 in 2012.[21] Elance, in fact, predicts that professional services will be "America's next great export."[22]

Another growing trend is the formation of virtual global teams. Ninety-four percent of employers in one recent survey said that, in the future, most businesses will use blended teams of online and on-site workers, while 95% agreed that soon, skills, not location, will determine who gets hired. Fifty-eight percent plan to double their spending on online workers in 2013.[23]

Technology has rendered the market for talent truly global. You may find yourself competing for work with similar professionals from around the world—a daunting prospect, especially when these workers can do the same things you can for less money. The key to survival is distinguishing yourself and offering something no one else can deliver. As *The World Is Flat* author Thomas Friedman puts it, "plain vanilla" won't cut it anymore: You need to set yourself apart by discerning and marketing your unique blend of skills, talents, and experience.[24]

Prosperity and Opportunity

But globalization brings opportunity as well as competition. Now, enterprising individuals and companies have vast new markets to sell to. Globalization has led to an increased standard of living for hundreds of millions of people. The global poverty rate has been cut more than in half since 1981,[25] and 35 million people worldwide joined the middle class between 2003 and 2009.[26] China's middle class is now larger than the US population.[27] This increased prosperity is shifting the balance of global economic power. Very broadly speaking, developed nations, particularly the United States and Japan, are losing their economic dominance, while developing nations, especially China and India, have growing clout. Since 2009, in fact, emerging nations have made up half the world's economy.[28] In 2012, 117 companies based in developing countries appeared on the *Fortune* Global 500 list, compared with just 13 in 1999.[29]

Companies have raced to do business in these promising markets. IBM expects to earn 30% of its revenue in developing countries by 2015, up from 17% in 2009, and Unilever already does 56% of its business in emerging regions.[30] The opening of global markets represents tremendous opportunity for companies large and small: Ninety-six percent of the world's population and three-quarters of its spending power exists outside the United States.[31]

And it's not only giant corporations that are profiting from globalization. Enterprising individuals and small firms are also entering new markets. Sites like eBay, Etsy, ArtFire, Ruby Lane, and Storenvy make setting up a global e-commerce store almost as simple as starting a blog. Business-to-business trading platform Alibaba connects small importers and exporters from over 240 countries. Logistics providers like FedEx and UPS allow small and medium-sized enterprises (SMEs) to trade overseas without having to establish sales teams and distribution networks.[32] These advances have led to steady growth in the extent of SMEs' participation in the global economy. SMEs accounted for 30% of US merchandise exports between 1997 and 2007,[33] and the number of US small exporters has more than doubled since 1992.[34] By 2018, half of US SMEs are expected to participate in global trade.[35]

Complexity and Competition

Doing business has gotten vastly more complex since globalization took hold, as the number of partners, collaborators, and competitors any company has to deal with has increased exponentially. More and more countries now have the resources, drive, and knowledge needed to compete for knowledge work on a global level. Brazil has become a hotbed of digital collaboration,[36] South Korea of digital media and genomics, and China of nanotech and biotech.[37] Companies in more developed nations have been forced to become more innovative and cut costs to stay competitive.

Many firms now outsource business functions to external providers, a process known as *disaggregation*. These providers may be US-, foreign- or multinationally based. A company might hire UPS to synchronize its global supply chain, for instance, or Evalueserve in India to perform market research for its medical or technical devices.[38] A decade ago, disaggregation mainly meant offshoring manufacturing to nations with lower labor costs. But disaggregation has become a much more complex phenomenon than simple outsourcing. When hiring service providers from abroad, companies do not merely choose the lowest bidder, but take into account such factors as quality, cultural similarities and differences, shipping costs, and time zones. Recently, North American companies have been looking to Latin America, and Western European firms to Eastern Europe, for business solutions, a phenomenon dubbed *nearsourcing*.[39] Though high- and medium-skilled workers in countries like Argentina and Poland may cost more than those in India, they often, employers say, have a greater understanding of how to interact with clients and a higher level of problem-solving skill.[40]

Disruptive innovations are also increasing the complexity of global business. Advances in 3D printing and robotics may bring advanced manufacturing jobs back to the US.[41] Rethink Robotics has invented a robot called Baxter with the capacity to perform repetitive work, adapt to changes in its environment, and work safely alongside humans. At $22,000, Baxter is affordable even for small manufacturers.[42]

Advances in telecommunications and transportation have allowed companies to create global supply chains and source materials, goods, and services from the producers who best meet their needs regardless of location. Savvy supply chain management can save businesses money, decrease time to market for goods, and increase customer satisfaction. Spanish fashion retailer Zara, for example, a master of supply chain management, is able to bring styles from runways to stores in just a matter of weeks by manufacturing some of its lines in Asia and others in nearby European and North African countries. Though the clothes made closer to headquarters are more costly to produce, they can be shipped more quickly and in smaller batches, so if items don't sell well, Zara doesn't lose much money on them. The higher labor costs incurred by sourcing clothes in Europe are offset by greater flexibility.[43] However, global supply chains have considerably increased the number of variables companies need to deal with, involving as they do everything from cultural, language, and time zone differences to unpredictable events such as strikes, political uprisings, and natural disasters.

This new complexity means workers will need to be adaptable and willing to change if they are to stay employed. In a rapidly changing global climate, you can't rest content with the status quo. Instead, anticipate and even welcome changes to your department, company, or entire industry. Keep abreast of trends in your industry and of global events which may affect your firm. In particular, stay informed about which skills are in demand, and be prepared to continually upgrade your skill set.

Longevity

In 1800, a 60-year-old would have been considered elderly. Today, that's middle-aged—in fact, 40% percent of 60-year-olds agree with the statement "60 is the new 40."[44] Since 1950, life expectancy has risen by four years for women and five for men,[45] and, by 2050, the average American man is expected to live to see 83 to 86 while the typical woman can expect to reach 89 to 94.[46] Britain's Office for National Statistics has even projected that one-third of babies born in 2012 will live to 100.[47]

Such extreme longevity is already having an impact upon careers. With so many of today's workers living and staying healthier longer, the concept of retirement at 65 is now outdated. Many people will find themselves working long past that age, some out of necessity but others out of a desire to remain productive and stimulated into their 60s, 70s, and beyond. Longevity also means members of multiple generations often share the same workplace, which can be a source of tension, especially in companies whose policies have not changed to reflect new demographics.

Redefining Retirement
One consequence of extreme longevity is that individuals and companies have had to change the way they think about retirement. The traditional concept of re-

tirement, in which a person stops working entirely in his or her 60s and embarks upon a life of leisure, is largely an artifact of the early and mid-20th century, when individuals tended to have more physically demanding jobs and shorter lifespans. In 1930, for example, a person who reached the age of 65 could only expect to remain disability-free for nine more years. Today, in contrast, 65-year-olds have an average of 14 disability-free years ahead of them, and that number's expected to rise to 17 years within a decade.[48] Someone who leaves the workforce at 65 today has a good chance of spending the next 25 years retired, a prospect that few people find psychologically satisfying or economically feasible.[49]

Individuals will also find they have to work longer to support aging relatives, as well as to provide for themselves in lengthier old age. By 2050, people over 65 will comprise 21% of the US population.[50] Many members of this elderly population will require medical care and assistance with everyday activities, putting further strain on the healthcare system and the family members who take care of them. The dependency ratio, or the proportion of children and retired people to working adults, is expected to increase from 59:100 to 72:100 by 2050.[51] That means working adults will have to carry the additional financial, physical, and emotional burdens of caring for both young and old. As a result, workers will need to structure their careers to manage these added pressures, and employers will need to adjust their career development policies to take into account their employees' responsibilities at home.

Longer lifespans also mean that people need to work longer to afford retirement when it does occur, and, unfortunately, not many Americans are financially prepared for lengthy old age. Only 21% of 50- to 64-year-olds are very confident that their income and assets are enough to support them in retirement.[52] The recent recession has further eroded the retirement savings of many, causing employees to stay in the workforce longer than they predicted. In 2009, in the midst of the recession, over half of workers aged 50 to 64 contemplated delaying retirement, and 16% believed they would never be able to retire.[53] Those who did plan to retire predicted they would do so at 66—five years later than they anticipated in 2006.[54] A 2012 survey of over 3,000 managers showed similar results: The majority of respondents named 65 to 69 as the ages they were most likely to retire, while a remarkable 33% of managers from the Baby Boom generation stated they would not retire until after 70.[55]

Yet financial necessity isn't the only reason older workers decide to defer retirement. Many find work too intellectually and socially stimulating to give up. A 2004 survey of Baby Boomers found that over three-quarters intended to earn money in retirement, and two-thirds listed mental stimulation and challenge as the top reasons why.[56] These employees are choosing a variety of alternatives to full retirement, including part-time work; phased retirement (working in a reduced capacity in the same industry or for the same company prior to full retirement);

returning to the workforce after a period of retirement; mentoring, advising, or consulting; freelancing or working on a project basis; and, as we discuss in the next section, entire second careers. Now, only about half of all employees go directly from full-time work to not working.[57] In fact, as Marc Freedman, author of *Encore: Finding Work That Matters in the Second Half of Life*, justly notes, "retirement" is not really the correct term for a phase of life that so often includes work.[58]

One Long Lifetime, Many Careers

Already, Americans are working longer. Labor force participation rates for people in their 60s and 70s have risen steadily over the past 15 years, especially for women,[59] and the percentage of the workforce over 55 will likely reach 20% by 2020.[60] The World Health Organization estimates that, today, healthy 60-year-olds are physically capable of working until their mid-to-late 70s.[61]

This unprecedented longevity has increased the likelihood that individuals will have multiple careers in their lifetimes. In fact, this shift is already occurring: The Bureau of Labor Statistics has found that even Baby Boomers, a generation not known as job-hoppers, held an average of 11 jobs before reaching age 46.[62] Far fewer people hold long jobs than in decades past. In 1980, 51% of workers had been in their current job more than 10 years; by 2005, only 39% had such lengthy job tenure.[63] The typical worker today has held his or her current job for only 4.4 years.[64]

Enter the phenomenon of the *encore* career: a full-fledged second career that a person embarks upon in the latter half of his or her life. Anywhere from 5.3 to 8.4 million Americans have such careers, which can last for 10, 15, or even 20 years—enough time for a person to complete a full career cycle, including training, returning to school, maturing into a new position, and then stepping down.[65] Many encore careerists, having spent their first careers pursuing money and power, view their second careers as opportunities to serve others. One study found that half of people over 50 were interested in jobs that would help their communities, and that 60% planned to reorder their priorities to emphasize social justice.[66] Teaching, nursing, childcare, and working for nonprofits are all popular choices for encore careers. Other examples of encore careerists include a finance executive who became a superintendent of a low-income school district, a car salesman turned activist, and a former hospital executive who now works with the homeless.[67]

Older workers derive great satisfaction from their second careers: 84% describe them as extremely fulfilling, and 94% say their jobs allow them to make a difference.[68] Interest in encore careers, not surprisingly, is growing. Half of Boomers not currently in encore careers want to have one.[69]

Generations Collide

For the first time, members of four and even five generations coexist in the workplace: Baby Boomers, Generation Xers, and Millennials[70] comprise the majority of the workforce, but some representatives of the Silent Generation (born between 1928 and 1945)[71] have yet to retire, and Generation Z[72] teenagers are now landing their first jobs. These generations were influenced by different historical events and parenting styles, and often have widely divergent approaches to technology, communication, office etiquette, leadership, and learning, which can lead to intergenerational tension. Boomer bosses, for example, may not understand why their Millennial subordinates want so much feedback and coaching, while Millennials may be frustrated by Xer teammates' preference for email over instant messaging. Sixty percent of HR professionals at large corporations report witnessing conflict between members of different generations.[73]

The mix of generations in the workplace has also forced employers to rethink career development and succession planning. The recent recession has caused many Boomers to delay retirement, much to the frustration of Xers, who had hoped to take over departing Boomers' leadership positions. Millennials expect rapid career advancement and may choose to leave a company if they aren't making as much progress as they'd hoped.

But having multiple generations in one workplace can also set the stage for rich transfers of knowledge and experience. Many older employees enjoy mentoring younger ones. Boomers and Millennials, for example, tend to share a love for self-expression, challenge, and new experiences, and can be especially effective mentor-mentee pairs.[74] Some companies even practice reverse mentoring, in which younger employees teach older ones about technology and how to market to younger generations.[75] The variety of perspectives brought about by generational diversity can also spark innovation. Eighty-two percent of HR professionals say the interaction of multiple generations leads to better quality work.[76]

The Generations at Work

Working with members of different generations can be challenging as well as invigorating. Learning about the work styles and motivations of each generation can help you better understand, manage, or collaborate with your colleagues.

Naturally, individuals differ, and not everyone shares the characteristics associated with his or her generation. But researchers have noted some general tendencies manifested by members of different generations, especially in regard to how they behave in the workplace. Here, in a nutshell, are some of the career issues facing each generation.

Baby Boomers: Vital Well Past Middle Age

Born during the years 1946 and 1964, and influenced by the idealism of the 1960s, Baby Boomers have refused to accept traditional working patterns. Many are staying in the workplace past typical retirement age: some due to financial necessity, but others because they cherish the intellectual stimulation and sense of purpose that work provides. Long considered hardworking, ambitious, and driven,[77] Boomers do tend to place a high value on work. They are almost twice as likely as members of younger generations to be work-centric as opposed to family-centric or equally concerned with work and family.[78]

Yet, as their interest in socially redeeming encore careers demonstrates, Boomers want more from work than salaries and titles. Studies have revealed that Boomers value flexibility, recognition, access to new experiences, opportunities to give back to society, and working with respected colleagues more than they do compensation.[79] Boomers also need flexibility as much as employees with young children do. They constitute a "sandwich generation": one simultaneously taking care of both older and younger family members. Seventy-one percent of Boomers have eldercare responsibilities while 41% provide financial support to young adult children.[80]

Well-educated and in good health, Boomers tend not to view themselves as "old" or "aging"; some scholars claim that Boomers experience a "second middle age" between 60 and 80.[81] Forty-seven percent of Boomers say they are only in the middle of their careers, and 68% expect to be promoted once more before retiring.[82] Eighty-five percent desire new experiences at work.[83]

Companies are struggling to cope with Boomers' lengthy working lives. Many Generation Xers find themselves unable to advance because Boomers still hold top positions. When Boomers, the largest generation in American history, do retire, they will leave a leadership gap in their wake as there are not enough qualified Xers to replace them. Companies must carefully craft succession plans to ensure that Boomers' experience and knowledge are not lost, and that younger workers are prepared to take their places.[84] Many have implemented initiatives such as phased retirement programs, mentoring programs, and opportunities for retired and semi-retired employees to contribute through mentoring, consulting, or short-term assignments.[85] Others are retaining Boomers longer by offering them the kinds of career development programs usually granted to younger workers, such as job rotations and opportunities for project-based work, which satisfy Boomers' thirst for knowledge and new experiences.[86]

Generation Xers: Frustration in Mid-Career

Born between 1965 and 1980, Generation Xers grew up during troubled times. Events like Watergate in 1972, the Gulf War in 1990–91, and the recession of the 1990s, which put many of their parents out of work, eroded their trust in authority. [87] Forty percent of Xers saw their parents divorce. Many had working mothers, and fully expect that they or the women in their lives will pursue careers; growing up as "latchkey kids" also fostered their independence.[88]

The "slacker" label affixed to Xers in the 1990s has proved unfounded. Xers are extremely hardworking. Thirty-one percent have "extreme jobs" requiring long hours and 24/7 availability, and 28% work 10 more hours a week than they did three years ago.[89] They're also entrepreneurial: 39% of Xer men and 28% of Xer women aspire to own their own businesses.[90] Such key Internet players as Amazon, Wikipedia, Google, and YouTube were all founded by Xers.

Generation Xers, having seen how hard their Silent Generation and Boomer parents worked, are committed to work-life balance. Fifty-two percent describe themselves as family-centric rather than work-centric or equally committed to work and family,[91] and many would choose better work-life balance options over higher salaries if given the choice,[92] partly because many are currently raising young children.

Xers are in or reaching the prime years of their careers, and are poised to replace exiting Baby Boomers in leadership positions. However, many of them are unsatisfied with their opportunities for advancement, partly because Boomers are staying in the workforce so long. Forty-nine percent of Xers say they feel "stalled" in their careers,[93] and 37% plan to leave their current employers in the next three years.[94] Over a fifth were actively job hunting in the past year.[95]

To retain Xers, companies may need to rethink their career development strategies. But not all Xers have the same needs. While many are clearly hungry for career advancement, others prefer flexible working arrangements to perks such as bonuses.[96] In fact, in keeping with their self-reliant spirit, Xers are more likely to pursue individualized careers than members of other cohorts.[97] Individualized career development options like mass career customization may be key to keeping this generation engaged.

Millennials: Hyperconnected and Ambitious

Millennials, born between 1981 and 1993, grew up in a world saturated with technology. Often called "digital natives," Millennials excel at multitasking, and using communications technology is second nature to them. Three-quarters of them have a social media profile, versus 50% of Xers and only 30% of Boomers,[98] and at work, 41% of them prefer to communicate electronically rather than face-to-face or over the phone.[99] A hyperconnected generation, they are heavy users of mobile devices who see little distinction between work and home life.[100]

Raised by highly involved parents who enriched their development by enrolling them in sports, classes, and other adult-organized activities, Millennials tend to value structure and frequent feedback on the job.[101] Achievement-oriented (they were the first generation to receive trophies for participation) Millennials also expect to move quickly through the ranks at work. Fifty-two percent name fast career progression as the quality that most attracts them to an employer.[102] "Millennials expect much faster advancement than the typical corporation expects to provide," says Nancy Sullivan, senior vice president at Lee Hecht Harrison. "Many young people look at colleagues in their 50s and wonder why it took so long for them to get where they are."

Survey: Boomer Job Seekers Pursue Skill Development, Gen Xers Want Higher Salaries

A 2013 survey of job seekers performed by national staffing firm Juststaff revealed some key differences in what Baby Boomers and Generation Xers are looking for in their next jobs.* Job security was both Boomers' and Xers' top priority, with 33% of Boomers and 35% of Xers naming it as the most important attribute they sought in a job. However, Boomers appear to value opportunities for skill development somewhat more than Xers, whereas Xers value salary slightly more. Thirty-one percent of Boomers and 25% of Xers named opportunities for experience and skill development as the criterion they most sought in a job, and 12% of Boomers and 18% of Xers named salary as their important criterion.

Likewise, Xer job seekers were more likely than Boomers to name salary and dislike for their current job as reasons why they were on the job market. Sixty-five percent of Boomers said they were seeking jobs because they were out of work, compared to only 47% of Xers. Twenty-two percent of Xers said they were looking for work to increase their salary, versus only 10% of Boomers, while 15% of Xers said they were seeking work because they disliked their current job, versus 6% of Boomers.

These findings may reflect Boomers' and Xers' different life stages. Many Xers may be looking to increase their income because they're raising children, or because they are in mid-career and believe they should earn more, while Boomers may be more willing to stay put as they're contemplating retirement. The results may also indicate broader generational differences regarding loyalty towards employers: Boomers may be less likely to leave a job unless they're forced out, whereas Xers may be more likely to leave an employer for what they consider a better deal.

* In Juststaff surveys, Baby Boomers are defined as those born between 1943 and 1960, Generation Xers as those born between 1961 and 1981, and Millennials as those born between 1982 and 2004.

"Younger workers need faster promotions, more rewards, and greater mobility than older ones," says Megan Remark, vice president at not-for-profit HMO HealthPartners. "They tend to move around more than Baby Boomers: After they've learned all they can from an experience, they want to move on." This desire for rapid advancement can sometimes cause friction between Millennials and their employers.

Millennials are family-oriented and idealistic. In one survey, 51% of Millennials said the most important thing in life is being a good parent, and 30% said having a successful marriage was most important. Only 15% named having a high-paying career as most important.[103] Millennials also view their careers as opportunities to give back to society, and are drawn to employers who share their values.[104]

Millennials are already a crucial demographic in the workforce, and are one that will only grow in importance. Almost as large a generation as the Baby Boomers, they will comprise nearly half the workforce by 2014.[105] They may also be the most educated generation in history: A record 40% of 18-to-24-year olds were enrolled in college in 2008.[106]

To recruit and retain the best Millennial talent, companies need to offer a mix of what this generation most desires: technology, flexibility, and opportunities for development. Millennials want to be able to use social media at work, and see little reason why they can't work remotely. Eighty-nine percent desire flexibility,[107] and two out of five would accept a lower-paying job offering flexibility and access to mobile technology and social media over a higher-paying one without these perks.[108] Accustomed to structure, Millennials also value clear-cut career paths,[109] and one-third name training and development as the benefit they most desire from an employer.[110] "Millennials resemble the Silent Generation in that they respond well to structure," says Sullivan. "They don't push back against authority and they want to know what the boundaries are."

Looking Ahead: Generation Z

The leading edge of Generation Z, or those born between 1993 and 2010, has just begun to enter the workplace. This generation has never known a world without the Internet, and they're even more technology dependent than Millennials. They grew up with social media, mobile devices, and online gaming, and they consider traditional television and email old-fashioned, far preferring texting and video-on-demand.[111] Seventy-nine percent of 13- to 15-year-old girls own mobile devices, and 81% of Gen Z members prefer blended or online education to learning from books alone.[112]

The Gen Z cohort inhabits a post–9/11 world and has never known a time when the United States was not at war. Media coverage of terrorism, global warming, and the recession has many of them uncertain about the future.[113] They are also one of the most sheltered and carefully parented generations in history, and, as a result, they are similar to the Silent Generation in their respect for authority and desire for security.[114]

Though it's too early to say exactly how Generation Z will respond to the workplace, in certain ways they can be expected to behave like more intense versions of Millennials: constantly connected, highly tech savvy, and desirous of clearly defined career paths.

Diversity

Perhaps part of the appeal of *Mad Men* is the way it acts as a time capsule, giving us a window into a workforce very different from our own. It's rather remarkable to look back at how, during a time within the living memory of many people, the majority of the white-collar workforce consisted of white men married to homemakers. Today, of course, the workplace is markedly different. Women hold 51% of all managerial and professional positions.[115] People of color now comprise 37% of the population,[116] and immigrants, many of them small business owners, form 13%.[117] Only 20% of American families consist of a working father, a stay-at-home mother, and their children.[118]

These demographic changes cannot help but change the way we think about careers. Now that so many women are in the workforce, for instance, it's no longer taken for granted that wives will be the ones to stay home to raise children. Both men and women are carefully considering how they will balance work and family life—and devising a wide range of working options in the process. Women are also leading the change from linear to labyrinthine careers by choosing entrepreneurship, freelancing, part-time work, encore careers, and other alternatives to corporate work at faster rates than men. Increased diversity is improving companies' ability to innovate, as women, minorities, and people with widely varying work, learning, and leadership styles bring their unique perspectives to the workplace.

Ethnic Diversity

In *Hospital: Man, Woman, Birth, Death, Infinity, Plus Red Tape, Behavior, Money, God, and Diversity on Steroids*, a chronicle of a year at Brooklyn's Maimonides Medical Center, author Julie Salamon describes a workplace in which the staff hails from all over the world and the "customers" speak 67 different languages. Obstetrics residents learn to count to 10 and say "push" in five different languages, including Cantonese and Russian. Hospital practices are continually tweaked to accommodate cultural differences. For instance, when the staff discovered that white sheets disturbed recent immigrant patients from China, where the color white is associated with death, they refitted all the hospital beds with beige sheets.[119]

Though Maimonides Medical Center may be exceptionally diverse (hence the "on steroids" portion of the title), it represents the way the American workforce is headed: towards ever-increasing diversity. The United States becomes a more variegated nation daily. People of color will form the majority of the population by 2050.[120] By that year, the Latino population is expected to grow from 19% to 30%, the Asian population from 5% to 9%, and the African American population from 12% to 13%,[121] and one in five citizens will be an immigrant.[122] (In 1980, in contrast, the US workforce was overwhelmingly—82%—Caucasian. By 2020, just 63% of the workforce will be white.[123]) Workers at all types of companies will interact with colleagues, superiors, customers, and competitors who hail from a wide variety of ethnic backgrounds, and will need to develop cultural competence and even foreign language skills.

A Nation of Immigrants

When many Americans hear the term "immigration," they remember history lessons about Irish, German, Polish, Russian, and other European migrants arriving at Ellis Island. Our children and grandchildren, though, will learn about another great wave of immigration—the one that's taking place right now. In the past four decades, 40 million immigrants have become American citizens in the most expansive period of immigration in US history.[124]

Unlike the European immigrants of the early 20th century, most of today's immigrants are Latino or Asian.[125] In fact, in 2009, Asians surpassed Latinos as the ethnic group most likely to emigrate to the United States.[126] Because members of these populations have higher birth rates and more women of childbearing age than the aging native Caucasian population, they're making a significant contribution to the changing racial makeup of the nation. Immigrants and their descendants are expected to account for 82% of population growth between 2005 and 2050.[127]

These new immigrants are a varied population, and they're making an impact on diverse areas of the workforce. Asian immigrants, for example, tend to be highly educated—61% hold bachelor's degrees—and to take jobs in high-paying fields like science, engineering, medicine, and finance.[128] Many Hispanic immigrants start businesses. The number of Latino-owned small businesses jumped 44% between 2002 and 2007.[129] As a whole, immigrants have higher rates of entrepreneurship than the native-born population. Eighteen percent of small business owners are immigrants, and the rate is much higher in some regions: 45% of small business owners in Miami and one-third of those in the state of California are immigrants.[130]

Today's employees will almost certainly be working alongside, selling to, or buying from people who were not born in the United States, may not have English as a first language, and may be transitioning between American business practices and customs and those of their countries of origin. Employers will also want to be sure their staff has the cultural competency and diversity to work well with America's increasingly varied population. California's population, for example, is 40% Latino, but Hispanics are underrepresented in its healthcare workforce (only 5% of physicians are of Latino descent), a situation which can lead to language barriers and cultural misunderstandings.[131] "We want our employee population to be more reflective of our patient population," says Remark, "so one way we recruit is by networking with organizations that represent groups prominent in that population." Having diverse employees can also help companies understand, market to, and recruit from different subgroups. "If you don't recruit from diverse groups of people, your employee base won't reflect the global consumer," observes Karen Robinson, senior director of human resources at the Apollo Group.

Women

In 2010, women reached a milestone, overtaking men to form the majority of the US workforce.[132] If current trends continue, they may comprise the majority of the leadership pipeline as well. Women already hold 51.4% of managerial and professional jobs and almost half of all banking and insurance jobs, and are 45% of associates in law firms.[133] Plus, they're pursuing higher education at a far faster rate than men, and now receive 57% of all college degrees and a slight majority of advanced and professional degrees.[134] Americans are also ready to see more women in leadership positions: 89% are comfortable with women as leaders.[135] Generation Xers and Millennials, the first generations whose mothers worked primarily outside the home, see no reason why women shouldn't fully participate in the workforce. Daughters of mothers who worked full time are more likely to plan to have uninterrupted careers, and sons of working mothers prefer that their spouses work full time.[136]

The new majority of women in the workforce will have striking consequences on the workplace, most of them positive. The transformational and relational leadership style preferred by many women, for instance, is well-suited to today's more connected and collaborative style of working.[137] Women are also helping to redefine traditional career paths, as many of them choose working options that take them outside the corporation, such as self-employment and starting their own businesses. Driven by value-oriented definitions of success, many women prioritize intellectual fulfillment, giving back to society, and attaining work-life balance above salary and status.[138] To retain female talent, including highly educated future female leaders, organizations may need to rethink their career development and reward strategies, taking into account the values that motivate their workers, and provide employees with more opportunities for flexibility and customized career paths.

The Rise of the Female Entrepreneur

One key way women are reshaping the landscape of careers is by starting businesses. Flickr, Blurb, Spanx, Build-A-Bear, PC Connection, the Body Shop—all these well-known brands were founded by women. But women own some 8.1 million other US firms as well.[139] No mere niche market, women-owned businesses have an annual economic impact of $3 trillion and employ 23 million people, or 16% of the US workforce.[140] If American women-owned businesses were their own country, it would have the fifth largest GDP in the world, ahead of France, the United Kingdom, and Italy.[141] Women are also starting businesses at a faster rate than men. The number of women-owned businesses increased 50% between 1997 and 2001, twice the rate of male-owned firms.[142] Between 1997 and 2007, companies owned by women added 500,000 jobs while other privately held firms lost over 2 million jobs,[143] and, by 2018, women-owned small businesses will create a projected 5 to 5.5 million jobs.[144]

In their propensity for entrepreneurship, women reflect the movement towards greater freedom, flexibility, and individualization in career paths. There are almost as many motivations for starting businesses as there are female business owners. While some women become entrepreneurs as a way of attaining greater work-life balance or control over their working lives, others are interested in implementing an idea, solving a problem through their companies, or fulfilling a dream of being their own boss. For example, Aihui Ong founded Love With Food, a company that sends customers samples of gourmet food from small producers, because she wanted to make food her life's work and because she was dissatisfied with her previous career as an engineer. Sherry Gunther started Masher Media because she saw opportunity in the growing market for online children's entertainment. Nurse Kristy Chambers launched consulting firm Medical Simulation Design with partner Jane Kleinman after they realized that healthcare organizations needed assistance with implementing new technologies.[145] For all these women, business ownership represented an alternative to traditional employment that fit their career paths.

The Right Leadership Style for the 21st Century

Companies with more women board members see 53% higher returns on equity, 42% higher returns on sales, and 66% higher returns on invested capital.[146] Firms that promote more women have 18% higher than average profits as a percentage of assets, 34% higher profits as a percentage of revenue, and 69% higher profits as a percentage of stockholders' equity.[147] Corporate boards with two or more female members are more likely to review customer and employee satisfaction and the implementation of strategy than all-male boards,[148] and companies with three or more women directors enjoy better organizational health.[149]

What explains these striking findings? In part, women's leadership style. Many women practice what's known as *transformational leadership*: a way of leading that focuses on mentoring and coaching rather than commanding and controlling. Transformational leaders take a keen personal interest in their followers' professional development, helping them to build their skills and reach their goals. They value the sharing of knowledge, solicit ideas from employees at all levels of their organizations, and ensure that everyone's voice is heard. Transformational leaders also create powerful visions that they inspire others to embrace and support.

As companies move away from hierarchical forms of organization to flatter, more egalitarian ones, leaders will need to adopt a more transformational style. They'll also need excellent relational skills to manage teams in the collaborative and project-based environment favored by many future-forward companies, and to shepherd employees through the change and uncertainty that have become characteristic of today's workplace. Women, a recent study finds, have the emotional intelligence needed to thrive as 21st-century leaders. In a survey of more than 3,100 male and female managers, respondents reported that women outperformed men on several key leadership traits, including empathy, problem solving, ethics/transparency, collaboration, and communication.[150]

But evidence shows that women also excel at "hard" leadership skills. On a 360-degree performance study by the Society for Human Resource Management, for example, women outscored men on 42 out of 52 executive competencies, including adaptability, driving execution, shaping strategy, and visionary thinking.[151] An Australian study determined that women executives scored higher than men on six of eight categories—including strategic drive, risk taking, people skills, innovation, and "hot buttons" or motivators—and tied men on one (emotional stability).[152]

Families

In 1950, 63% of American families followed the traditional "nuclear" pattern of a husband who worked and a wife who stayed home to care for the children.[153] As late as 1975, 45% of families still maintained this structure.[154] In that year, only 10% of women ages 40 to 44 had never had a child,[155] and only 39% of women with children under six were in the workforce.[156]

Today's families are far more diverse. Only 20% can be considered traditional, in the midcentury sense.[157] The others represent a mosaic of working, marital, and child-rearing choices, and include dual-income couples with or without children, single and divorced parents, stay-at-home fathers with working spouses, gay and lesbian couples, and multigenerational and single-person households. The 2010 census reveals just how dramatically the American family has changed. In that year, for the first time since records were kept in 1940, the percentage of households incorporating a married couple fell below 50% for the first time, while the percentage of all other types of households increased (see Figure 1.1).[158]

Generation and Gender

Evolving gender roles are responsible for much of the change in American family dynamics. Most Generation Xers and Millennials saw their mothers work outside the home, and therefore don't view housework and childcare as women's domain. Instead, they expect that women will work and men will perform their share of the household duties. As a result, the number of couples who both work has skyrocketed. Eighty percent of married or partnered employees belong to dual-income households.[159] And more women have become primary breadwinners. In 2009, almost four out of 10 working wives outearned their husbands, and if this trend continues, more families will be supported by women than men in the next generation.[160] In most large US cities, women under 30 already make more money than men the same age.[161]

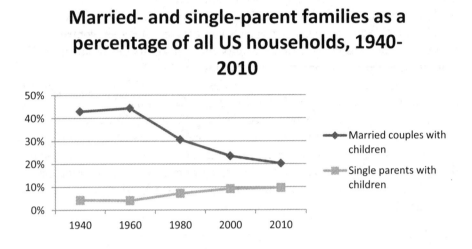

Figure 1.1. Source: Linda A. Jacobsen, Mark Mather, and Genevieve Dupuis, *Household Change in the United States* (Washington, DC: Population Reference Bureau, 2012), 3, http://www.prb.org/pdf12/us-household-change-2012.pdf.

Meanwhile, many Generation X and Millennial men are embracing involved fatherhood. Not content to merely be breadwinner dads, they're actively nurturing and mentoring their children. Millennial men spend an average of 4.1 hours per workday with their kids, unlike their counterparts in 1977, who spent only 2.4 hours with them.[162] Ninety-four percent of fathers say they'd consider how taking a new job would affect their children, and 77% say they'd like to spend more time with their kids on workdays.[163]

And young men are more open to caring for their children full time. Fifty-three percent would be open to becoming stay-at-home dads if it was economically feasible. The number of stay-at-home fathers is small, but it has more than doubled over the past decade.[164] Men are also devoting more time to household chores, with 55% reporting they do an equal or greater share of cooking for the families and 53% saying the same about cleaning.[165] As a result, men now report *higher* levels of work-life conflict than do women.[166]

The Multigenerational Family—and Household
Americans' increased longevity is also reshaping the family unit and changing how families spend their time. Millions more adults now have eldercare responsibilities. In the past three months, almost 40 million Americans reported providing unpaid care to someone over the age of 65, typically a family member. The vast majority of these caretakers are of working age. Around 23% of people ages 45 to

---

Survey: Male and Female Job Seekers
Are Both in Search of Job Security

A 2013 survey of job seekers sponsored by national staffing firm Juststaff found that both men and women prioritize security when searching for jobs. Both men and women named security the attribute they most wanted in their next job, with 34% of men and 33% of women choosing it as their top option. Similar percentages of men and women—16% and 18%, respectively—named a higher salary as their top criterion for a new job.

However, 32% of men but only 24% of women stated having opportunities for experience and skill development were most important to them in their next job, whereas 13% of women but only 7% of men named better benefits as most important.

Men and women had strikingly similar reasons for seeking work. Fifty-three percent of men and 49% of women said they were looking for a job because they did not currently have one, while 18% of both men and women had jobs but were pursuing positions with higher salaries, and 13% of both men and women said they disliked their current jobs and were searching for something new.

These results suggest that men may be somewhat more concerned with their career development when searching for their next job, given their slightly higher tendency to prioritize experience and skills, while women may be somewhat more interested in immediate, tangible benefits such as salary and health insurance.

---

64 care for an elderly person. The one out of every eight 40- to 60-year olds who are caring for both minors and elderly relatives are doubly strapped. Most must struggle to balance work and heavy family responsibilities.

Longevity has contributed to another growing trend: the return of the multi-generational household. Around the time of World War II, 25% of Americans lived in such households, but by 1980 only 12% did. But multigenerational households are on the rise due to trends such as older people moving in with their children, younger people delaying marriage, young adults "boomeranging" back to live with their parents for economic reasons, and an increase in immigrants from countries where such living arrangements are more common. Sixteen percent of Americans now live with at least two other generations of family members.[167]

These changes to family dynamics have led to changes in career patterns, in part because many large companies' policies do not align well with employees' needs for flexibility. There's still a tacit assumption that the ideal employee is one who is totally available to the company, working plenty of overtime, rarely taking time off, and dropping everything to travel at a moment's notice.[168] Naturally, it's a lot easier to live up to this ideal if you don't have children or elderly family members to take care of, or if you're married to someone who can take care of them for you. Up to 90% of companies' policies are still calibrated to traditional family patterns.[169]

Workplace culture and practices have, by and large, not kept pace with changes in earning patterns and gender roles. Family-oriented Gen X and Millennial men, for instance, are as interested in work-life balance options as women, but are less likely to request them for fear of appearing less than committed to their jobs.[170] Too often, flexible working arrangements are viewed as "mommy track" options indicative of divided loyalties, even though men, single people, and older workers as well as mothers express interest in them. Forty percent of working parents fear their jobs would be in jeopardy if they took advantage of flexible working arrangements, and only 24% of men and 33% of women think they could turn down a promotion for family reasons without being viewed negatively.[171]

Partly as a result of companies' inflexible schedules and policies, more people today are choosing alternatives to corporate employment, or opting to work for corporations only during the stages of their lives when they have the most time and energy to devote to their careers. Some choose alternatives to linear career advancement including switching industries, making lateral moves, starting their own businesses, freelancing or becoming self-employed, taking time off for family or personal reasons, working part time, or re-entering the corporate world after working outside it. (We'll discuss these myriad options in greater detail in Chapter 2.)

Women are in the forefront of the movement away from traditional careers. They're more likely than men to have these unconventional career paths: 58% of highly qualified women describe their careers as nonlinear,[172] and 45% of women change jobs, start businesses, or consider doing so at midlife.[173]

Though rearing children is a primary reason women seek alternatives to traditional jobs, it's far from the only one. In fact, just 35% of women who leave the workforce name childcare as their *sole* reason for doing so.[174] Women also cite needs for greater challenge, balance, and accomplishment, and a desire for work that aligns with their values, as key reasons for pursuing labyrinthine careers. Forty-six percent of women describe success as "personal fulfillment or happiness," a much higher percentage than view success in terms of recognition or financial reward.[175] Women are also likely to see work and life not as isolated spheres but as intertwined, a viewpoint that, as we've seen, is prevalent among Gen Xers and Millennials of both genders. Half of women describe the relationship between their professional and personal lives as integrated, and a further 39% say it is moving towards integration. The blurring of boundaries between work and home may also explain why so many women choose customized career paths and seek creative working alternatives: to be more fulfilled and balanced.

Men, too, are beginning to reconfigure their career patterns to better integrate work and family life. For instance, it's recently become more acceptable for men to stay home with their children. Fifty-three percent of fathers say they would consider staying home if their spouse made enough money to support them.[176] There are an estimated 147,000 stay-at-home dads in the United States, though this estimate is likely low because it does not include the many stay-at-home fathers who work part time.[177] The number of stay-at-home dads has increased threefold in Canada over the past 30 years.[178] Like working mothers, stay-at-home fathers find many creative ways to balance work and home lives, such as working part time or becoming self-employed. They typically re-enter the workforce once their children are old enough, and may alternate time off with their spouses. Some mothers, for instance, stay home for their babies' first year of life, after which they return to work while their husbands take care of the children.[179]

Work-Life Balance: Not Only for Parents
Households composed of single people and couples without children have, like almost every other type of living arrangement, grown in number in recent years. The number of single-person households, in fact, has steadily increased for the past six decades, driven by delayed marriage, growing divorce rates, and the rising elderly population. Only 14% of Americans lived alone in 1960; in 2011, 28% did. And, as choosing not to have children becomes more widely accepted (41% of Americans say children are "very important" to a successful marriage, down from 65% in 1990[180]), more couples are opting not to become parents. Forty-three percent of Gen X women and almost a third of Gen X men do not have children.[181] Twenty percent of women ages 40 to 44 have never given birth, including 27% of women with graduate and professional degrees.[182]

Though single and childless employees may have fewer family responsibilities and perhaps more time to devote to their careers, they, too, are voicing needs for greater work-life balance. Some are leaving high-pressure jobs for freelance or contract-based work precisely because they want greater control over their schedules and more time for volunteering, exercise, education, relaxing, socializing, hobbies and creative pursuits, and other aspects of their very full lives.[183] Millennial women without children, studies show, value work-life balance as much as Millennial moms,[184] and mothers and non-mothers both cite the need for balance as a key reason for switching jobs. Employers, however, may not be paying sufficient attention to single employees' need for flexibility: 62% of singles say they are treated differently on the job than workers with families, and 35% feel they are perceived as lacking responsibilities.[185]

Putting It Together: VUCA

Technology, globalization, diversity, longevity, demographic factors, increased competition from around the world—all these forces combined have made doing business, as well as planning careers, more complicated than ever before. Today's companies have to tackle vaster and thornier problems than they have previously faced. Consider what it takes, for example, to implement an international supply chain. A firm might need to take into account not only price and quality but such factors as:

- Language, culture, and religion (Who'll communicate with suppliers, and in what language? Can you expect delays around Ramadan or Chinese New Year?)

- Politics (What are the risks of hiring a supplier in a politically unstable country?)

- Weather, climate, and natural disasters (How will monsoon season affect your shipping routes?)

- Energy (Who'll absorb the cost if fuel prices increase?)

- Labor relations (What happens to your deliveries if the truckers' union goes on strike? Do your suppliers provide fair wages and working conditions?)

- Economics (What if one of the countries in your supply chain is hit by a recession? How much will your prices be affected if the dollar's weak against the euro or the RMB?)

- Public relations (If the press discovers one of your suppliers is subcontracting to sweatshops, how will your company respond?)

In an IBM survey of over 1,500 CEOs from 33 industries in more than 60 countries, 79% said they foresaw business becoming even more complex in the future.[186] In fact, the new business climate has become so unstable that writers have adopted an acronym from the Army War College to describe it: VUCA, which stands for *V*olatile, *U*ncertain, *C*omplex, and *A*mbiguous.[187]

In a VUCA world, companies need to be lean, agile, and innovative to stay competitive. They have to streamline operations, continually evaluating legacy processes and eliminating or tweaking those that are no longer optimal. They must scan the environment for signs of incipient change, particular in regard to competitors and disruptive innovations. And they must innovate, quickly developing new products, services, and ways of relating to customers in response to shifting conditions.[188] CEOs in the IBM survey named creativity—not assertiveness, vision, or experience—as the most important characteristic for leaders to possess.[189]

And the same is true of employees. To succeed in a VUCA world you'll need to be innovative, informed, alert to changes in your environment, and open to change. Companies seek employees who can help them stay afloat in an uncertain market: flexible creative thinkers who continually add to their skill sets and knowledge bases. To increase your chances for success in a VUCA workplace, try the following tips:

- *Reject the status quo.* Expect change. In fact, embrace it. Technological innovations, new competitors, political or economic happenings abroad— all can change your industry, your company, or your role in an eyeblink. Stay informed about trends in your field so they don't catch you off guard. Evaluate the currency and portability of your skills. Be an early adopter. Plan for your next career or role while you're still in your current one.

- *Embrace lifelong learning and skill development.* As you can expect to have many jobs and even multiple careers over the course of your working lifetime, be prepared to continually learn new skills and information. You can do so formally, through earning degrees and certificates or taking classes, or informally, by attending seminars and conferences in your field, reading the latest books and articles about your industry, or taking advantage of the wealth of tutorials and how-to videos available on the Internet.

- *Cultivate an entrepreneurial mindset.* With so much competition, it's important that you learn to market yourself. Develop a personal brand. Determine what makes you unique and make it your main selling point.

- *Be financially prudent.* In an age of increased longevity, you'll likely need to train for a second career, and, when you do retire, it'll probably be for a longer period of time. You'll need money put away for all these possibilities. Having a little extra in the bank can also give you added peace of mind in case you want to make a career transition, or if a life change such as the birth of a child or the illness of a family member forces you into one.

- *Be a hybrid worker.* As technology permeates more and more fields, and as scientific and technical companies become more consumer-oriented, jobs have come to require a blend of both hard and soft skills. If you work in a people-oriented industry, become conversant with key technologies; if you're in a technical field, you can make yourself a more valuable employee by developing your communication and collaborative skills.

- *Become T-shaped.* The problems faced by today's companies are so complex they must be addressed by experts in multiple disciplines Many firms now expect employees to break out of their silos and function well on interdisciplinary teams. *T-shaped* workers have deep knowledge of one subject (the vertical bar of the "T") and shallower knowledge of a broad variety of subjects (the horizontal bar of the "T"). To become a T-shaped individual, cultivate knowledge from fields outside your own that pertain to your job. If you're a marketing professional at a pharmaceutical firm, for example, learn something about medicine, chemistry, public health, or health insurance. You don't have to be an expert: The key is to be able to speak the same "language" as colleagues in other disciplines. Learn how people in those disciplines think, communicate, generate new ideas, and test hypotheses, what their main concerns and goals are, and what trends are current in their field.[190]

- *Expect to have a borderless career.* Today's employees should view themselves as competing against workers all over the world. But it's also likely that they'll be working with people from other countries and even taking on international assignments. McKinsey predicts that, by 2020, global mobility will become "the new normal" as companies develop talent abroad and relocate workers.[191] To prepare for such global careers, you should cultivate such competencies as a global mindset, cultural intelligence, strategic thinking, and adaptability.[192] Keep yourself well-informed about global politics, world affairs, and cultural differences.[193] Consider taking expatriate assignments, which are "amazing for development," suggests Elizabeth,* who was formerly an executive working in business development for a Silicon Valley-based coaching firm. Katherine Markgraf, assistant director of executive recruiting–tax at Ernst & Young, says her company offers one-year rotations to other countries. "Our employees return with many ideas we can implement in the US market," she says.

Notes

1. Henry Helgeson, "The Best Weapon That Merchants Have to Combat 'Showrooming,'" *Business Insider*, April 28, 2013, http://www.businessinsider.com/how-to-fight-showrooming-2013-4.
2. Rick Aristotle Munarriz, "5 Bricks-and-Mortar Retailers That Are Showrooming-Proof," *DailyFinance*, June 26, 2012, http://www.dailyfinance.com/2012/06/26/5-bricks-and-mortar-retailers-that-are-showrooming-proof/.
3. Samantha Murphy, "Retailers Turn 'Showrooming' Into Innovation Opportunity," *Mashable*, May 19, 2013, http://mashable.com/2013/05/19/showrooming/; Monica DeBois, "Showrooming: The New Wave of Retail Shopping," *The Inside Scoop* (blog), *Media Works*, March 15, 2013, http://mediaworksltd.wordpress.com/2013/03/15/showrooming-the-new-wave-of-retail-shopping/; Helgeson, "The Best Weapon."
4. Damon Lavrinc, "Apple, Google Just Killed Portable GPS Devices," *Wired*, June 12, 2012, http://www.wired.com/autopia/2012/06/gps-devices-are-dead/.
5. Jeanne C. Meister and Karie Willyerd, *The 2020 Workplace: How Innovative Companies Attract, Develop, and Keep Tomorrow's Employees Today* (New York: HarperBusiness, 2010), Kindle edition, chap. 1.

---

* Name changed at the interviewee's request.

6. Mary Madden and Kathryn Zickhur, *65% of Online Adults Use Social Networking Sites* (Washington, DC: Pew Research Center, 2011), 2, http://www.ucsf.edu/sites/default/files/legacy_files/PIP-SNS-Update-2011.pdf.

7. Rick Edmonds et al., "Newspapers: By the Numbers," *The State of the News Media 2012*, accessed August 6, 2013, http://stateofthemedia.org/2012/newspapers-building-digital-revenues-proves-painfully-slow/newspapers-by-the-numbers/.

8. Jeff Jarvis, "Newspapers in 2020," *BuzzMachine* (blog), September 6, 2007, http://buzzmachine.com/newspapers-in-2020.

9. Enrico Moretti, *The New Geography of Jobs* (Boston: Houghton Mifflin Harcourt, 2012), Kindle edition, chap. 2.

10. Ibid.

11. "Cloud Computing to Create 14 Million New Jobs by 2015," Microsoft, March 5, 2012, http://www.microsoft.com/en-us/news/features/2012/mar12/03-05CloudComputingJobs.aspx.

12. *Wikipedia*, s.v. "Facebook," last modified June 7, 2013, http://en.wikipedia.org/wiki/Facebook; *Wikipedia*, s.v. "eBay," last modified June 7, 2013, http://en.wikipedia.org/wiki/Ebay; *Wikipedia*, s.v. "Google," last modified June 6, 2013, http://en.wikipedia.org/wiki/Google.

13. James Manyika and Charles Roxburgh, *The Great Transformer: The Impact of the Internet on Economic Growth and Prosperity* (Washington, DC: McKinsey Global Institute, 2011), 1, http://www.mckinsey.com/insights/mgi/research/technology_and_innovation/the_great_transformer.

14. Moretti, *New Geography of Jobs,* chap. 2.

15. Meister and Willyerd, *2020 Workplace,* chap. 1.

16. John Hagel III, John Seely Brown, and Lang Davison, "Abandon Stocks, Embrace Flows," *Harvard Business Review*, January 27, 2009, http://blogs.hbr.org/bigshift/2009/01/abandon-stocks-embrace-flows.html.

17. Thomas L. Friedman, *The World Is Flat: A Brief History of the Twenty-First Century*, 2nd ed. (New York: Farrar, Straus and Giroux, 2006), 243.

18. Lynda Gratton, *The Shift: The Future of Work Is Already Here* (London: HarperCollins, 2011), 25.

19. Jessica Stillman, "Elance's Impressive Growth: Good News for Its US Users?" *Gigaom,* December 7, 2011, http://gigaom.com/2011/12/07/elances-impressive-growth-good-news-for-its-us-users/.

20. Jessica Stillman, "Elance Predicts the Future of Online Work," *Gigaom,* March 27, 2012, http://gigaom.com/2012/03/27/elance-predicts-the-future-of-online-work/.

21. oDesk, "oDesk Announces Global Study of More Than 2,800 Businesses Indicating Significant Disruption of Traditional Hiring Model as Online Work Soars," news release, October 9, 2012, https://www.odesk.com/info/about/press/releases/odesk-announces-global-study/.

22. Stillman, "Elance's Impressive Growth."

23. oDesk, "oDesk Announces Global Study."

24. Friedman, *World Is Flat*, 102–4.

25. Daniel Griswold, "Opening the World of Export Opportunity to US Small Businesses" (statement before the Committee on Small Business, United States House of Representatives, June 19, 2008), http://www.cato.org/testimony/ct-dg-20080619.html?q=/node/885.

26. Deloitte, *Human Capital Trends 2012: Leap Ahead* (New York: Deloitte, 2012), 6, http://www.deloitte.com/assets/Dcom-UnitedStates/Local%20Assets/Documents/us_cons_hc-trends12_022312.pdf.

27. Ibid.

28. Gratton, *Shift*, 73.

29. "Index to the Fortune Global 500," *CNNMoney,* August 2, 1999, http://money.cnn.com/magazines/fortune/fortune_archive/1999/08/02/263627/index.htm; "Global 500. Full List. 2012," *CNNMoney,* July 23, 2012, http://money.cnn.com/magazines/fortune/global500/2012/full_list/.

30. Martin Dewhurst, Suzanne Heywood, and Jon Harris, "The Global Company's Challenge," *McKinsey Quarterly,* June 2012, https://www.mckinseyquarterly.com/The_global_companys_challenge_2979.

31. Griswold, "Opening the World."

32. Ibid.

33. US International Trade Commission, *Small and Medium-Sized Enterprises Overview of Participation in US Exports,* Investigation No. 332-508, USITC Publication 4125, January 2010, ix, http://www.usitc.gov/publications/332/pub4125.pdf.

34. Griswold, "Opening the World."

35. Steve King, Anthony Townsend, and Carolyn Ockels, *Intuit Future of Small Business Report. Second Installment: Technology Trends and Small Business* (Palo Alto, CA: Institute for the Future for Intuit, 2007), 24, http://http-download.intuit.com/http.intuit/CMO/intuit/futureofsmallbusiness/SR-1037B_intuit_tech_trends.pdf.

36. Lee-Sean Huang, "Four Lessons from the Social Innovation Hotbed of Brazil," *Co.EXIST* (blog), *Fast Company,* accessed November 20, 2012, http://www.fastcoexist.com/1679295/4-lessons-from-the-social-innovation-hotbed-of-brazil.

37. Gratton, *Shift,* 189-90.

38. Pete Engardio, with Michael Arndt and Dean Foust, "The Future of Outsourcing," *Businessweek,* January 29, 2006, http://www.businessweek.com/stories/2006-01-29/the-future-of-outsourcing.

39. John Helyar, "Outsourcing: A Passage out of India," *Businessweek,* March 15, 2012, http://www.businessweek.com/articles/2012-03-15/outsourcing-a-passage-out-of-india.

40. Kathleen Hall, "Why More Businesses Are Nearshoring in Eastern Europe," *ComputerWeekly,* July 2011, http://www.computerweekly.com/feature/Why-more-businesses-are-nearshoring-in-Eastern-Europe.

41. Jeremy Hsu and TechNewsDaily, "Why 3-D Printing Matters for 'Made in U.S.A.,'" *Scientific American,* December 6, 2012, http://www.scientificamerican.com/article.cfm?id=why-3d-printing-matters.

42. Erico Guizzo and Evan Ackerman, "How Rethink Robotics Built Its New Baxter Robot Worker," *IEEE Spectrum,* October 2012, http://spectrum.ieee.org/robotics/industrial-robots/rethink-robotics-baxter-robot-factory-worker.

43. Seth Stevenson, "Polka Dots Are In? Polka Dots It Is!," *Slate,* June 21, 2012, http://www.slate.com/articles/arts/operations/2012/06/zara_s_fast_fashion_how_the_company_gets_new_styles_to_stores_so_quickly_.html.

44. Marc Freedman, *Encore: Finding Work that Matters in the Second Half of Life* (New York: PublicAffairs, 2008), Kindle edition, chap. 4.

45. Joseph F. Quinn, "Work, Retirement, and the Encore Career: Elders and the Future of the American Workforce," *Generations* 34, no. 3 (2010): 48.

46. Lauren Cox, "We Will Live Longer in 2050, Study Predicts," *ABC News,* December 14, 2009, http://abcnews.go.com/Health/ActiveAging/humans-live-longer-2050-scientists-predict/story?id=9330511#.UaKEukDCaSo.

47. Sam Jones and Maev Kennedy, "More Than a Third of Babies Born in 2012 Will Live to 100, Report Predicts," *Guardian,* March 26, 2012, http://www.guardian.co.uk/society/2012/mar/26/third-babies-2012-live-100.

48. Freedman, *Encore,* chap. 2.

49. Gratton, *Shift,* 251.
50. Paul Taylor, Cary Funk, and Peyton Craighill, *Working After Retirement: The Gap Between Expectations and Reality* (Washington, DC: Pew Research Center, 2006), 1, http://www.pew-socialtrends.org/files/2010/10/Retirement.pdf.
51. Jeffrey Passel and D'Vera Cohn, *U.S. Population Projections: 2005–2050* (Washington, DC: Pew Research Center, 2008), ii, http://www.pewsocialtrends.org/files/2010/10/85.pdf.
52. Pew Research Center, *Most Middle-Aged Adults Are Rethinking Retirement Plans* (Pew Research Center: Washington, DC, 2009), http://www.pewsocialtrends.org/2009/05/28/most-middle-aged-adults-are-rethinking-retirement-plans/.
53. Ibid.
54. Taylor, Funk, and Craighill, *Working After Retirement*, 1; Pew Research Center, *Middle-Aged Adults Rethinking Retirement Plans.*
55. Tracey Wilen-Daugenti, Courtney L. Vien, and Caroline Molina-Ray, eds., *Women Lead: Career Perspectives from Workplace Leaders* (New York: Peter Lang, 2013), 25–26.
56. Quinn, "Work, Retirement, and the Encore Career," 51.
57. Kevin H. Cahill, Michael D. Giandrea, and Joseph F. Quinn, "Reentering the Labor Force after Retirement," *Monthly Labor Review*, June 2011, 34; Suzanne M. Bianchi, "Changing Families, Changing Workplaces," *The Future of Children* 21, no. 2 (2011): 36.
58. Freedman, *Encore,* chap. 4.
59. Quinn, "Work, Retirement, and the Encore Career," 49.
60. Meister and Willyerd, *2020 Workplace,* chap. 2.
61. Ibid., introduction.
62. US Bureau of Labor Statistics, "Number of Jobs Held, Labor Market Activity, and Earnings Growth Among the Youngest Baby Boomers: Results from a Longitudinal Study," news release, July 25, 2012, http://www.bls.gov/news.release/pdf/nlsoy.pdf.
63. Anya Kamenetz, "The Four-Year Career," *Fast Company*, February 2012, http://www.fastcompany.com/1802731/four-year-career.
64. Ibid.
65. Peter D. Hart Research Associates, *Encore Career Survey* (New York: MetLife Foundation/Civic Ventures, 2008), 5, http://www.civicventures.org/publications/surveys/encore_career_survey/Encore_Survey.pdf.
66. Freedman, *Encore*, chap. 1.
67. Ibid.
68. Peter D. Hart Research Associates, *Encore Career Survey*, 6.
69. Ibid., 4.
70. Names for this generation differ, with some scholars dubbing them Generation Y or the Net Generation.
71. Though there is rough consensus on the time period each generation was born, not all researchers assign the same birth years to the same generations. In this book, we use the same designations as Pew Research Center, one of the leading organizations studying generational differences.
72. This generation has yet to acquire a widely accepted moniker. Other names suggested for it include Generation@, the Net Generation, the iGeneration, the Homeland Generation, and the Pluralist Generation.
73. Judi Casey and Barbara Denton, "Effective Workplace Series. Work-Family Information on: Generation X/Generation Y," *Sloan Work and Family Research Network*, March 2008, https://workfamily.sas.upenn.edu/sites/workfamily.sas.upenn.edu/files/imported/pdfs/EWS_GenXandY.pdf.

74. Sylvia Ann Hewlett et al., *Bookend Generations: Leveraging Talent and Finding Common Ground* (New York: Center for Work-Life Policy, 2009): 41–46.

75. Families and Work Institute, *Tips for Managers: Generation & Gender in the Workforce* (New York: Families and Work Institute, 2009), 1, http://familiesandwork.org/site/research/reports/GG-managertips.pdf.

76. Jason Dobbs et al., *The Multi-Generational Workplace* (Chestnut Hill, MA: The Sloan Center on Aging & Work at Boston College, 2007), 2, http://www.bc.edu/content/dam/files/research_sites/agingandwork/pdf/publications/FS09_MultiGenWorkplace.pdf

77. Meister and Willyerd, *2020 Workplace,* chap. 2; Josh Bersin, "A New Organizational Learning Model: Learning On-Demand," *Bersin by Deloitte* (blog), October 1, 2007, http://joshbersin.com/2007/10/01/a-new-organizational-learning-model-learning-on-demand/.

78. Dobbs et al., *Multi-Generational Workplace*, 2.

79. Hewlett et al., *Bookend Generations*, 2.

80. Ibid., 35.

81. Ibid., 38.

82. Ibid., 3.

83. Ibid., 2.

84. Families and Work Institute, *Tips for Managers*, 1.

85. Hewlett et al., *Bookend Generations*, 38.

86. Ibid., 39.

87. Sylvia Ann Hewlett and Lauren Leader-Chivée, *The X Factor: Tapping into the Strengths of the 33-to-46-Year-Old Generation* (New York: Center for Work-Life Policy, 2011),11; Gratton, *Shift*, 96.

88. Meister and Willyerd, *2020 Workplace,* chap. 2.

89. Hewlett and Leader-Chivée, *X Factor*, 1.

90. Ibid., 11.

91. Sloan Work and Family Research Network, "Questions and Answers About Generation X/Generation Y: A Sloan Work & Family Research Network Fact Sheet," accessed January 3, 2013, http://workfamily.sas.upenn.edu/sites/workfamily.sas.upenn.edu/files/imported/pdfs/GXGY.pdf.

92. Tamara Erickson, "Don't Treat Them Like Baby Boomers," *Businessweek,* August 13, 2008, http://www.businessweek.com/stories/2008-08-13/dont-treat-them-like-baby-boomers.

93. Hewlett and Leader-Chivée, *X Factor*, 18.

94. Ibid., 1.

95. Ibid., 18.

96. Ibid., 33–41.

97. Diane Thielfoldt and Devon Scheef, "Generation X and the Millennials: What You Need to Know About Mentoring the New Generations," *Law Practice Today,* November 2005, http://apps.americanbar.org/lpm/lpt/articles/mgt08044.html.

98. Pew Research Center, "Millennials: Confident. Connected. Open to Change," February 24, 2010, http://www.pewsocialtrends.org/2010/02/24/millennials-confident-connected-open-to-change/.

99. PricewaterhouseCoopers, "Managing Tomorrow's People. Key Findings," accessed January 3, 2013, http://www.pwc.com/gx/en/managing-tomorrows-people/future-of-work/key-findings.jhtml.

100. Meister and Willyerd, *2020 Workplace,* chap. 2.

101. Neil Howe and William Strauss, *Millennials Rising: The Next Great Generation* (New York: Vintage, 2000), Kindle edition, introduction.

102. PricewaterhouseCoopers, "Managing Tomorrow's People."

103. Ibid.

104. Hewlett et al., *Bookend Generations*, 2.

105. Meister and Willyerd, *2020 Workplace*, introduction.

106. Pew Research Center, "Millennials."

107. Hewlett et al., *Bookend Generations*, 2.

108. Cisco, *The Future of Work: Information Access Expectations, Demand, and Behavior of the World's Next-Generation Workforce* (San Jose, CA: Cisco, 2011), presentation slides, 5, http://www.cisco.com/en/US/solutions/ns341/ns525/ns537/ns705/ns1120/cisco_connected_world_technology_report_chapter2_press_deck.pdf.

109. Jennifer Sabatini Fraone, Danielle Hartmann, and Kristin McNally, *The Multi-Generational Workforce: Management Implications and Strategies for Collaboration* (Chestnut Hill, MA: Boston College Center for Work & Family, 2007), http://www.bc.edu/content/dam/files/centers/cwf/research/publications/pdf/MultiGen_EBS.pdf; Meister and Willyerd, *2020 Workplace*, chap. 2.

110. Ibid.

111. Grail Research, *Consumers of Tomorrow: Insights and Observations About Generation Z* (Cambridge, MA: Grail Research, 2011), http://www.grailresearch.com/pdf/ContenPodsPdf/Consumers_of_Tomorrow_Insights_and_Observations_About_Generation_Z.pdf; Bruce Tulgan, "High-Maintenance Generation Z Heads to Work," *USA Today*, June 26, 2012, http://usatoday30.usatoday.com/news/opinion/forum/story/2012-06-27/generation-z-work-millenials-social-media-graduates/55845098/1.

112. Grail Research, *Consumers of Tomorrow*.

113. Grail Research, *Consumers of Tomorrow*; Tulgan, "High-Maintenance Generation Z."

114. Tulgan, "High-Maintenance Generation Z."

115. Hanna Rosin, "The End of Men," *The Atlantic*, July/August 2010, http://www.theatlantic.com/magazine/archive/2010/07/the-end-of-men/8135/1/.

116. Paul Taylor and D'Vera Cohn, "A Milestone En Route to a Majority Minority Nation," Pew Research Center, November 7, 2012, http://www.pewsocialtrends.org/2012/11/07/a-milestone-en-route-to-a-majority-minority-nation/.

117. UPI.com, "U.S. Immigrant Population 40.4 Million," January 29, 2013, http://www.upi.com/Top_News/US/2013/01/29/US-immigrant-population-404-million/UPI-59191359490020/.

118. Brad Harrington, Fred Van Deusen, and Beth Humberd, *The New Dad: Caring, Committed and Conflicted* (Chestnut Hill, MA: Boston College Center for Work and Family, 2011), 3, http://www.bc.edu/content/dam/files/centers/cwf/pdf/FH-Study-Web-2.pdf.

119. Julie Salamon, *Hospital: Man, Woman, Birth, Death, Infinity, Plus Red Tape, Bad Behavior, Money, God, and Diversity on Steroids* (New York: Penguin, 2008), Kindle edition, prologue.

120. Paul Taylor and D'Vera Cohn, "Majority Minority Nation."

121. Ibid.

122. Passel and Cohn, *U.S. Population Projections: 2005–2050*, i.

123. Meister and Willyerd, *2020 Workplace*, chap. 2.

124. Taylor and Cohn, "Majority Minority Nation."

125. Ibid.

126. Pew Research Center, *The Rise of Asian Americans* (Washington, DC: Pew Research Center, 2012), 20, http://www.pewsocialtrends.org/files/2012/06/SDT-The-Rise-of-Asian-Americans-Full-Report.pdf.

127. Passel and Cohn, *U.S. Population Projections: 2005–2050*, 1.

128. Pew Research Center, *Rise of Asian Americans*.

129. US Census Bureau, "Census Bureau Reports Hispanic-Owned Businesses Increase at More Than Double National Rate," news release, September 21, 2010, http://www.census.gov/newsroom/releases/archives/business_ownership/cb10-145.html.

130. Fiscal Policy Institute, *Immigrant Small Business Owners: A Significant and Growing Part of the Economy* (New York: Fiscal Policy Institute, 2012), 1, 4, http://fiscalpolicy.org/immigrant-small-business-owners-FPI-20120614.pdf.

131. Apollo Research Institute, *The Future of Work* (Phoenix, AZ: Apollo Research Institute, 2012), 3, http://apolloresearchinstitute.com/sites/default/files/future_of_work_report_final.pdf (site discontinued).

132. "The Rich World's Quiet Revolution: Women Are Gradually Taking Over the Workplace," *The Economist,* December 30, 2009, http://www.economist.com/node/15174489

133. Hanna Rosin, "End of Men."

134. Ibid.

135. White House Project, *The White House Project: Benchmarking Women's Leadership* (Brooklyn, NY: The White House Project, 2009), 7-8, http://thewhitehouseproject.org/wp-content/uploads/2012/03/benchmark_wom_leadership.pdf.

136. Susan M. Bosco and Candy A. Bianco, "Influence of Maternal Work Patterns and Socioeconomic Status on Gen Y Lifestyle Choice," *Journal of Career Development* 32, no. 2 (2005): 175.

137. Wilen-Daugenti, Vien, and Molina-Ray, eds. *Women Lead,* 25-26.

138. Ibid., 121–22.

139. American Express, *The American Express OPEN State of Women-Owned Businesses Report* (New York: American Express, 2011), 2, http://media.nucleus.naprojects.com/pdf/WomanReport_FINAL.pdf.

140. Center for Women's Business Research, *The Economic Impact of Women-Owned Businesses in the United States* (McLean, VA: Center for Women's Business Research, 2009), 1, http://www.womensbusinessresearchcenter.org/Data/research/economicimpactstud/econimpactreport-final.pdf.

141. Ibid.

142. US Department of Commerce Economics and Statistics Administration, *Women-Owned Businesses in the 21st Century* (Washington, DC: US Department of Commerce Economics and Statistics Administration, 2010), 11, http://www.dol.gov/wb/media/Women-Owned_Businesses_in_The_21st_Century.pdf.

143. Ibid.

144. Guardian Life Small Business Research Institute, *Women Small Business Owners Will Create 5+ Million New Jobs by 2019, Transforming the Workplace for Millions of Americans* (New York: The Guardian Life Small Business Research Institute, 2009), 3, http://www.smallbizdom.com/glife11pp/groups/camp_internet/@stellent_camp_website_smallbizdom/documents/report/women-small-business-owners.pdf.

145. Wilen-Daugenti, Vien, and Molina-Ray, *Women Lead,* 66, 71–72.

146. Lois Joy et al., *The Bottom Line: Corporate Performance and Women's Representation on Boards* (Princeton, NJ: Catalyst, 2007), http://www.catalyst.org/file/139/bottom%20line%202.pdf.

147. Roy D. Adler, "Profit, Thy Name Is . . . Woman?" *Pacific Standard,* February 27, 2009, http://www.psmag.com/business-economics/profit-thy-name-is-woman-3920/.

148. David A. H. Brown, Debra L. Brown, and Vanessa Anastasopoulos, *Women on Boards: Not Just the Right Thing . . . But the "Bright" Thing* (Ottawa: The Conference Board of Canada, 2002), 5, 12–13, http://www.europeanpwn.net/files/women_on_boards_canada.pdf.

149. Georges Desvaux, Sandrine Devillard-Hoellinger, and Pascal Baumgarten, *Women Matter: Gender Diversity, A Corporate Performance Driver* (Paris: McKinsey & Co., 2007), 14, http://www.europeanpwn.net/files/mckinsey_2007_gender_matters.pdf.

150. Wilen-Daugenti, Vien, and Molina-Ray, *Women Lead*, 90.

151. Global Human Capital Gender Advisory Council, *The Leaking Pipeline: Where Are Our Female Leaders? 79 Women Share Their Stories* (London: PricewaterhouseCoopers, 2008), 15, http://www.pwc.com/en_GX/gx/women-at-pwc/assets/leaking_pipeline.pdf.

152. Peter Berry, Shayne Nealon, and Kim Pluess, *Female Leadership in Australia* (Northbridge, Australia: 2008), 8–10, http://www.peterberry.com.au/files//white_papers/pbc_white_paper_-_female_leadership_in_australia_berry_nealon__pluess.pdf. Men scored higher than women on control-and-command leadership and bottom-line thinking.

153. Cathleen Benko and Anne Weisberg, *Mass Career Customization: Aligning the Workplace with Today's Nontraditional Workforce* (Cambridge, MA: Harvard Business School, 2007), 2.

154. Harrington, Van Deusen, and Humberd, *New Dad*, 3.

155. Bianchi, "Changing Families, Changing Workplaces," 24.

156. Ibid., 16.

157. Harrington, Van Deusen, and Humberd, *New Dad*, 3.

158. Elizabeth Harrington, "Less Than 50% of U.S. Households Now Led by Married Couples, Says Census Bureau," *CNSNews.com*, April 25, 2012, http://cnsnews.com/news/article/less-50-us-households-now-led-married-couples-says-census-bureau.

159. Ellen Galinsky, Kerstin Aumann, and James T. Bond, *Times Are Changing: Gender and Generation at Work and Home* (New York: Families and Work Institute, 2011), 8, http://familiesandwork.org/site/research/reports/Times_Are_Changing.pdf.

160. Lisa Mundy, "Women, Money, and Power," *Time*, March 26, 2012, http://www.time.com/time/magazine/article/0,9171,2109140,00.html.

161. Catherine New, "Income Gap Closing: Women on Pace to Outearn Men," *Huffington Post*, March 21, 2012, http://www.huffingtonpost.com/2012/03/21/income-gap-women-make-more-men_n_1368328.html.

162. Galinksy, Aumann, and Bond, *Times Are Changing*, 15.

163. Harrington, Van Deusen, and Humberd, *New Dad*, 16.

164. Alex Williams, "Just Wait Until Your Mother Gets Home," *New York Times*, August 10, 2012, http://www.nytimes.com/2012/08/12/fashion/dads-are-taking-over-as-full-time-parents.html?pagewanted=all&_r=0.

165. Galinksy, Aumann, and Bond, *Times Are Changing*, 17–18.

166. Ibid., 18.

167. Paul Taylor, et al., *The Return of the Multi-Generational Family Household* (Washington, DC: Pew Research Center, 2010), 1, http://www.pewsocialtrends.org/files/2010/10/752-multi-generational-families.pdf.

168. Lauren Aguilar, "The Myth of the Ideal Worker: New Workforce, Outdated Workplace," *Gender News* (blog), Clayman Institute for Gender Research, April 16, 2012, http://gender.stanford.edu/news/2012/myth-ideal-worker-new-workforce-outdated-workplace.

169. Benko and Weisberg, *Mass Career Customization*, 7.

170. Ibid., 47.

171. Ibid., 62-3.

172. Sylvia Ann Hewlett and Carolyn Buck Luce, "Off-Ramps and On-Ramps: Keeping Talented Women on the Road to Success," *Harvard Business Review*, March 2005, 5, http://hbr.org/2005/03/off-ramps-and-on-ramps-keeping-talented-women-on-the-road-to-success/ar/1.

173. Betsy Morris and Ruth M. Coxeter, "Executive Women Confront Midlife Crisis," *Fortune*, September 18, 1995, http://money.cnn.com/magazines/fortune/fortune_archive/1995/09/18/206085/index.htm.

174. Elizabeth F. Cabrera, "Opting Out and Opting In: Understanding the Complexities of Women's Career Transitions," *Career Development International* 12, no. 3 (2007): 1, http://e-archivo. uc3m.es/bitstream/10016/11270/1/opting_cabrera_CDI_2007_ps.pdf.

175. Deborah O'Neil and Diana Bilimoria, "Women's Career Development Phases: Idealism, Endurance, and Reinvention," *Career Development International* 10, no. 3 (2005): 181.

176. Ibid., 17.

177. Elaine Bowers, "Dads Dive Into the Stay-at-Home Role," *ParentMap*, February 3, 2009, http://www.parentmap.com/article/dads-dive-into-the-stay-at-home-role.

178. May Jeong, "Number of Stay-at-Home Dads on the Rise," *Economy Lab* (blog), *Globe and Mail*, June 17, 2011, http://www.theglobeandmail.com/report-on-business/economy/economy-lab/ daily-mix/number-of-stay-at-home-dads-on-the-rise/article2065381/.

179. Bowers, "Dads Dive"; Kimberly Palmer, "The Rise of the Stay-at-Home Dad," *Alpha Consumer* (blog), *US News and World Report*, June 26, 2009, http://money.usnews.com/money/blogs/ alpha-consumer/2009/06/26/the-rise-of-the-stay-at-home-dad.

180. Pew Research Center, "Modern Marriage," July 18, 2007, http://www.pewsocialtrends. org/2007/07/18/modern-marriage/.

181. Hewlett and Leader-Chivée, *The X Factor*, 27.

182. Bianchi, "Changing Families," 24.

183. Sue Shellenbarger, "Single and Off the Fast Track," *Wall Street Journal*, May 23, 2012, http:// online.wsj.com/article/SB10001424052702304791704577420130278948866.html; Kate Bolick, "Single People Deserve Work-Life Balance, Too," *The Atlantic*, June 28, 2012, http:// www.theatlantic.com/business/archive/2012/06/single-people-deserve-work-life-balance-too/259071/.

184. Business and Professional Women's Foundation, *From Gen Y Women to Employers: What They Want in the Workplace and Why It Matters for Business* (Business and Professional Women's Foundation, 2011), 6, http://www.bpwfoundation.org/documents/uploads/YC_ SummaryReport_Final_Web.pdf.

185. Shellenbarger, "Single and Off the Fast Track."

186. IBM Institute for Business Value and IBM Strategy & Change, *Capitalizing on Complexity: Insights from the Global Chief Executive Officer Study* (Somers, NY: IBM Global Business Services, 2010), 8, http://public.dhe.ibm.com/common/ssi/ecm/en/gbe03297usen/GBE03297USEN. PDF; Institute for the Future for Apollo Research Institute, *Future of Work Report: The VUCA World* (Palo Alto, CA: Institute for the Future; Phoenix, AZ: Apollo Research Institute, 2011), 1, http://apolloresearchinstitute.com/sites/default/files/future-of-work-report-the-vuca-world. pdf (site discontinued).

187. Institute for the Future for Apollo Research Institute, *The VUCA World*, 1–2.

188. IBM Institute for Business Value and IBM Strategy & Change, *Capitalizing on Complexity*, 8–10.

189. Ibid., 8.

190. Institute for the Future for University of Phoenix Research Institute, *Future Work Skills 2020* (Palo Alto, CA: Institute for the Future; Phoenix, AZ: University of Phoenix Research Institute, 2011), 11, http://www.iftf.org/uploads/media/SR-1382A_UPRI_future_work_skills_ sm.pdf.

191. PricewaterhouseCoopers, *Talent Mobility: 2020 and Beyond* (London: PricewaterhouseCoopers, 2012), 3–4, http://www.pwc.com/en_GX/gx/managing-tomorrows-people/future-of-work/pdf/pwc-talent-mobility-2020.pdf.

192. Karen V. Beaman, *2011–2012 Going Global Report: HCM Trends in Globalization* (San Francisco: Jeitosa Group International, 2011), 14, http://www.jeitosa.com/wp-content/

uploads/2011/12/Going-Global-Report-HCM-Trends-in-Globalization-FINAL-IHRIMWire-DEC-2011-1-PGV.pdf.

193. Terrance Malkinson, "Globalization and Your Career: Building Career Resilience," *IEEE-USA Today's Engineer Online,* February 2006, http://www.todaysengineer.org/2006/Feb/globalization.asp.

CHAPTER TWO

From Ladder to Labyrinth

New Ways of Working and the Rise of the Do-It-Yourself Career

Walter was born in 1920. He received an engineering degree at age 22 and took a job with a textile firm in New England. Walter's talent was quickly recognized, and he was soon promoted to a management position. He spent the next 43 years with the same company, moving up the ranks. His job required him to move several times over the course of his career, and he spent much of his time on the road inspecting the company's mills, but, as his wife was a full-time homemaker, this did not present a hardship. When Walter retired at age 65, he had attained the rank of senior vice president.

Walter's daughter, Debbie, was born in 1954. She earned a nursing degree from a hospital-based diploma program, and went to work as a staff nurse for that same hospital. After she gained more experience, she was promoted to nurse manager. In the early 1990s, Debbie noticed that more of her younger colleagues had bachelor's degrees, and how their skills and knowledge helped them on the job. She enrolled in night school, earned a BSN, and found it so intellectually stimulating that she continued on for her master's degree. This degree enabled her to take a less physically demanding, but higher-paying, job as a case manager in her 50s. Debbie doesn't want to retire for at least 10 more years, but, when she does, she plans to volunteer for a nonprofit patient advocacy organization.

Debbie's daughter, Carly, was born in 1979. She received a bachelor's degree in journalism and became a staff reporter for a local newspaper. At that job, she discovered an interest in design and layout, earned a certificate in graphic design online, and was asked to design several special sections of the newspaper. In the early 2000s, the growth of the Internet took a heavy toll on the print news industry, and Carly lost her job when her paper went out of business. Her design portfolio, however, helped her to land a position with a small marketing and communications firm. After working there for a few years and building up a base of clients, Carly decided she wanted more flexibility over her time and the types of projects she worked on, and went into business for herself as an independent contractor. Her clients are scattered all across the country, and, as she mainly works online, she's never met most of them face-to-face. In her spare time, Carly is teaching herself web design as a way of adding value to her business.

The Do-It-Yourself Career Path

As these vignettes illustrate, the way we conceive of the career path has changed dramatically over the past few decades. The era of the gold watch—if it ever really existed to begin with[1]—is long over. Now, out of desire and necessity, more and more people are crafting customized careers, moving with increasing fluidity between corporate jobs, stints with small companies or nonprofits, self-employment, business ownership, part-time work, and time spent out of the workforce altogether. No longer do they feel constrained to remain within one industry for life: They may retrain or return to school, repackaging some of their skills and experiences and acquiring others, in preparation for work in affiliated or entirely new fields. Their career moves are dictated (for the most part) not by their employers but by their needs, values, and life circumstances. They may seek a new job or type of work, or ramp their workload and salary expectations up or down, due to having a child, needing to care for an elderly family member, pursuing an opportunity, wanting to learn a new skill or content area, or simply out of desire for change.

In this section, we'll discuss the shifts in priorities that brought about this fundamental alteration in the concept of the career path; the new trajectories careers now follow; the many options workers have for customizing their careers, both inside and outside the corporation; changes in the structure and hierarchy of the corporate workplace; and the skills and characteristics you'll need to successfully forge your own do-it-yourself career path.

Changing Priorities

The term "midlife crisis" has been part of the American lexicon since 1965.[2] As the stereotype goes, a midlife crisis occurs when an ambitious person reaches his (or sometimes her) forties, realizes that he's spent his entire adult life in pursuit of money and power, and undergoes a transformation. Perhaps he tries to recapture his lost youth by buying a fancy sports car, perhaps he becomes more spiritual and starts practicing yoga, or perhaps he simply vows to spend more time with his family.

Today, however, many workers never need to reach a crisis point: They let non-material values guide them from the beginning. Societal and demographic changes have brought about a shift away from work-for-work's-sake towards work as vocation. Though traditional motivators like security, salary, prestige, and advancement still drive many employees, they're increasingly seeking work that allows them to make a difference to society or to maximize their talents. Employees are also rejecting the concept of work and home as separate spheres, instead looking to integrate work with family life and leisure time.

Disenchantment with the structure and instability of corporate work has partly driven this shift in values. The boom-and-bust cycles of the early 2000s, and particularly the recession of 2008–9, which led many companies to lay off workers or go out of business altogether, have embittered many workers towards corporations.[3] They no longer trust companies to uphold their end of the employment deal by rewarding loyalty with security and opportunities for advancement. Between 2008 and 2009, years when the recession was in full swing, the percentage of employees who said their company lived up to its employment deal fell by 30%.[4]

The recession has also tarnished corporations' image—and this at a time when more workers care about corporate ethics. A PricewaterhouseCoopers study of recent college hires, for example, found that 86% would consider leaving an employer whose social responsibility quotient did not live up to their expectations.[5] Less than 60% of workers worldwide say their organizations are ethical and highly regarded by the public.[6]

Employees are also finding that corporations' values no longer dovetail with their own. They cite security, flexibility, and control over their own work as attributes they most desire in a job. Sixty percent of Americans who recently found jobs said they were likely to leave their employers if they did not provide sufficient flexibility.[7] Seventy-eight percent of workers say they can manage their work with little or no oversight.[8] Younger employees, in particular, care about a company's coolness factor—its brand name, status in its industry, and capacity for innovation.[9] Recent college hires list job mobility, training and development, overseas assignments, and mentoring as qualities they look for in an employer.[10]

But too few companies provide jobs with the characteristics workers most need. Perhaps as a result, job satisfaction worldwide is low. As a global survey by Towers Watson determined, only 35% of workers are highly engaged with their jobs. Seventeen percent are "detached," performing well but maintaining no emotional connection to their employers, while 26% are "disengaged," working only for salary.[11] Just under half of workers say their organizations' senior leaders are truly interested in their employees' well-being.[12]

Employee loyalty is likewise in decline. A 2012 MetLife survey found that employee commitment was at a seven-year low. One in three workers plans to leave his or her job by the end of the year, and 76% say they would leave their employer if the right opportunity came along.[13] Forty-three percent of American workers say they'll need to leave their firms to make progress in their careers.[14]

Redefining Success

But inflexible policies and a shaky economy are only part of the reason workers have become disenchanted with corporate employment. Employees are also reassessing their values, and determining that balance, self-actualization, and community service matter as much as money and prestige.[15] Forty-six percent of women, for example, describe success as "personal fulfillment or happiness," a much higher percentage than view success in terms of recognition or financial reward.[16] Millennials, who were raised to excel, seek work that allows them to grow as people,[17] while Boomers, as we've seen, pursue encore careers which enable them to serve others.

In particular, workers are carefully contemplating the impact of their career decisions upon their home and family lives. What's different now is that men as well as women are prioritizing work-life balance. Women have long tended to view work and life not as isolated spheres but as intertwining realms. Most women balance the demands of work with their own needs and those of their families, friends, and communities, and carefully evaluate the effects of their career decisions on the people who matter to them. They naturally see work and family life as overlapping realms that mutually influence one another.[18] Half of women say the relationship between their personal and professional lives is integrated, and a further 39% describe it as moving towards integration.[19]

But now, men too are placing a higher value on family life. Generation X and Millennial men are likely to decrease the hours they work after the birth of a child, unlike Baby Boomer men, who are more likely to *increase* the time spent at work.[20] A Radcliffe Public Policy Center survey found that 82% of young men consider family more important than increasing their salary or prestige at work.[21] Seventy-two percent of men say they would sacrifice higher pay and exciting opportunities at work for more time with their families.[22]

Men and women of all generations now seek more from work than a paycheck: They're looking for meaningful employment that allows them to maximize their talents, achieve personal growth, contribute to society, and spend more quality time with their friends and families. Too often, however, corporate employment does not foster these goals. Or employees may find working for a large company appealing at certain stages of their lives but not others. As a result, many workers have left corporations to forge their own unconventional career paths.

Changing Trajectories

An in-house editor for a small publishing firm becomes a contractor after she has a baby, giving her greater control over the hours she works. An advertising executive at a Fortune 500 company leaves to found her own niche marketing firm. An engineer returns to traditional corporate employment after a stint as an entrepreneur. A retiring vice president of sales retrains for an encore career as fundraising director at a nonprofit which works to protect endangered species, a cause he's long admired. A recent college graduate never works nine-to-five at all but jumps straight into a career as a freelance graphic designer.

As career moves like these become the norm, the way we conceive of the career path changes. Once, the dominant metaphors for the career path were the ladder and the bell curve. The ladder image, with its connotations of continuous upward movement, implied that employees were motivated primarily by a desire for advancement. The metaphor of the bell curve likewise suggested that the ideal employee's career would follow a predictable arc: from entry-level work in his 20s, to middle management in his 30s, to peak power and salary in his 50s, to a slow stepping back from responsibility until retirement in his 60s.[23] Neither the ladder nor the bell curve allows for career breaks, reversals, or second (or third) careers.

But, as we've seen, many individuals' careers do contain these elements. Thus, new metaphors have been developed to describe the career path, such as the lattice, the zigzag, and the labyrinth. Careers today are so unpredictable and individualized that some experts believe we should abandon spatial imagery altogether, and instead depict careers as boundaryless, protean, or kaleidoscopic. Though difficult to map, these new types of careers have certain things in common. They're driven by workers' values, needs, and desires rather than by companies' agendas. And the individuals who pursue them don't derive their identities from the firms they work for but from their skills, experiences, and personal characteristics.[24] They're not Apple IT specialists but IT specialists who happen to work for Apple—for now.

Boundaryless careers also change as workers' life circumstances change, helping weave work and home life into a more seamless whole. In fact, women, who shoulder the biological burden of pregnancy and traditionally have been expected to be the primary caretakers of children, have pioneered the movement towards the boundaryless career. Forty-one percent of women, versus only 21% of men, have made changes in their career for family reasons, and 29% of women change jobs or careers to achieve greater work-family balance, compared with 14% of men.[25] Fifty-eight percent of highly qualified women describe their careers as nonlinear,[26] and 45% of women change jobs, start businesses, or consider doing so at midlife.[27] Men, in contrast, are less likely to have interrupted careers, work part time, or change industries than women.[28] Twenty-six percent of men but only 18% of women say their careers both were linear and took place within the same industry.[29]

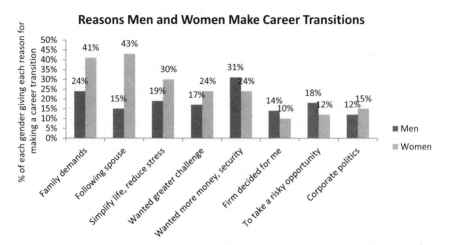

Figure 2.1. Source: Lisa A. Mainiero and Sherry E. Sullivan, *The Opt-Out Revolt: Why People Are Leaving Companies to Create Kaleidoscope Careers* (Mountain View, CA: Davies-Black, 2006), 310.

However, though rearing children is a primary reason women seek alternatives to traditional jobs, it's far from the only one (see Figure 2.1). In fact, just 35% of women who leave the workforce name childcare as their *sole* reason for doing so.[30] Women also step out of the workforce due to downsizing, medical crises, lack of challenging work, and to pursue education, among myriad other reasons;[31] their motivations for career transitions include travel, reducing stress, money, security, and new opportunities.[32]

Lisa Mainiero and Sherry Sullivan, authors of *The Opt-Out Revolt: Why People Are Leaving Companies to Create Kaleidoscope Careers*, observe that the trajectories of today's careers are often linked to gender. Different values, they posit, become primary at different points in may women's lives. Women tend to be most strongly motivated by the value of *challenge* in early career, when they seek advancement and are more willing to put their careers first. If they choose to become mothers, *balance* becomes their main driver as they seek work that will allow them flexibility for raising their children. *Authenticity* drives them after their children are older or leave home, when they have renewed energy for pursuing fulfilling work.[33]

Men, Mainiero and Sullivan say, have typically followed a different pattern, being driven by challenge in early career but seeking authenticity at mid-career, a time when they often reassess their values. Men tend to be driven by balance in late career, when they are contemplating retirement and view family as more of a priority. However, generational differences may be altering this pattern. Generation X and Millennial men, who tend to be more interested in hands-on fatherhood, have career patterns more similar to women.[34]

Changing Options

Workers now have more options than ever for putting together these do-it-your-self careers. No longer is working for a large corporation considered the surest route to success. Self-employed individuals may freelance, start businesses, or operate franchises, while employees of progressive companies have great flexibility in where and when they work and how much responsibility they want to shoulder, and those working for small- and medium-sized companies often find they have more opportunities for innovation. Public sector jobs often offer workers greater security and better benefits packages than large companies can, and jobs in the nonprofit sector enable them to give back to their communities, while providing ample room for advancement. Below, we take a closer look at many of these exciting options.

Beyond the Corporation

Large companies—those with revenues over $1 billion—are providing more flexibility and career path options all the time, and are empowering their workers through technology. But millions of people have recently chosen to pursue flexibility, freedom, and control over their work outside the boundaries of traditional employment by going to work for themselves. The numbers of both freelancers and entrepreneurs have risen dramatically over the past few years, largely because technology has lowered the bar for entry into self-employment. Freelancers can post portfolios online and instantly connect with potential employers all over the world, and small business owners can sell goods and services to almost anyone with an Internet connection. Economic and generational changes have also contributed to the self-employment boom. Many people who were laid off or had a hard time finding jobs during the recession turned to independent work to support themselves, and discovered they were more satisfied working on their own than for large companies. Value-driven and independent Generation Xers and tech-savvy Millennials also tend to find self-employment appealing, as do Boomers contemplating encore careers. All these factors have converged to make freelancing and entrepreneurship increasingly popular alternatives to traditional employment.

Freelancing

LiveOps's 20,000 employees are all contractors who work from home on a part-time, as needed basis.[35] Sites like oDesk and Elance bring together millions of independent contractors with the companies that want to hire them. The "gig economy" is taking off, and it's poised to experience even more rapid growth in the near future. Between 1995 and 2005, the number of self-employed people increased 37%, to almost nine million.[36] Now an estimated 12 million people freelance, and two million more are expected to join the contingent workforce by 2015.[37]

These independent workers run the gamut from creative types like graphic designers, writers, and photographers to professionals such as engineers, consultants, and IT specialists to temporary clerical or factory workers. Many are highly skilled. Forty-four percent hold bachelor's degrees, and 20% have master's degrees.[38] Their motivations for choosing self-employment vary widely. Some 14% to 17% turned to freelancing after being laid off or downsized, often during the recent recession.[39]

But, for increasing numbers of people, freelancing is a deliberately chosen career strategy: a valid alternative to, and not a substitute for, traditional employment. Many individuals turn to freelancing after becoming disenchanted with corporate life, or because they view it as an avenue to greater freedom and control over their work. In one national survey, 28% of freelancers named wanting a more flexible schedule as the main reason they became self-employed, while 23% said they did so to pursue a passion.[40] Most of those who had worked full time prior to going independent were satisfied with their decision. Ninety percent said they were happier than they had been as employees, 46% said they had more free time, and 55% said they'd never consider returning to traditional employment.[41]

Technology, more than anything, has made freelancing a viable career path. In the past, freelancers had to rely on word of mouth and distributing business cards and fliers to find jobs.[42] Now, they can easily create websites advertising their work, post professional multimedia portfolios online, use social media to network and promote themselves, search job boards or sites like Elance for gigs, and hire online services to handle their paperwork. The Internet has expanded their reach from their local area to the globe.

More work, too, is now available for freelancers, as companies have discovered that using contractors enables them to hire for just the skills they need, when they need them.[43] They may opt to bring in a marketing specialist, for example, to help them with a rebranding effort, or an expert in supply chain management to consult on a new product line. Hiring contractors spares organizations the expense and complexity of taking on full-time employees, making them more agile. In the future, more organizations will likely have "blended workforces" composed of both permanent and continent workers.[44] Fifty-eight percent of firms plan to use more temporary workers over the next five years,[45] and 40% say they can find better talent online than they can locally.[46] Using contractors can be especially advantageous for small and medium-sized businesses, 85% of which report that hiring online gives them a competitive edge.[47]

Freelance work is not without its drawbacks. Independent contractors must pay for their own health insurance and manage their own retirement savings, and they have fewer legal protections against problems such as wage theft.[48] Some freelancers feel less financially secure than they did as full-time employees, with 21% citing the "feast or famine" nature of contingent work as their biggest challenge.[49]

Others, though, note that having a diverse portfolio of clients protects them from the contingencies of the business world, as they aren't tied to the fortunes of one company.[50] Freelancers also have to develop entrepreneurial skills to be successful: They must be able to promote themselves, stay attuned to the market and anticipate its needs, maintain strong networks, create compelling personal brands, and carefully manage their professional reputations.

Entrepreneurship

As with freelancing, entrepreneurship has become more popular as an alternative to traditional employment in recent years. And it's no wonder why. Technology has made it easier than ever to start a business. Millions of people have set up shop on eBay, Etsy, and Amazon, or by simply starting a website and signing up for online financial transfer services like PayPal. Social networking and cost-efficient marketing tools like Google AdWords allow small business owners to reach broad, even worldwide, audiences; software, some of it free, enables them to handle everything from bookkeeping to invoicing to inventory control; and software-as-a-service frees them from heavy up-front infrastructure costs. Entrepreneurs can even use crowdfunding sites like Kickstarter and Indiegogo to seek capital.

As with freelancing, individuals cite varied reasons for going into business for themselves. Some have had a lifelong dream to own a business, while others feel that typical jobs didn't give them enough freedom or control over their schedules. Others turn to business ownership after being laid off or downsized. A good many entrepreneurs start out in corporate jobs, but become dissatisfied with traditional employment, want greater independence, or simply hatch an idea for a product or service they wanted to sell. Making the jump from traditional employment to entrepreneurship can be fruitful. According to one survey, 87% of successful entrepreneurs started their companies in areas where they already had business experience.[51]

Though interest in business ownership waned during the recent recession, it's making a comeback as the economy recovers. In 2011, 12% of working-age adults were starting or running a business, 60% more than did so in 2010. Nearly 40% of these business owners said they planned to hire five or more employees over the next five years.[52] Plus, if generational trends hold, the country may soon be seeing a surge in entrepreneurship. Between 1999 and 2009, Baby Boomers had the highest rate of business creation of any age group, starting firms at a rate one-third faster than younger people. Millennials, too, are avidly interested in entrepreneurships. They launched 160,000 startups a month in 2011,[53] and 54% of them say they have started or are considering starting a business.[54] Younger Americans' enthusiasm for business creation is reflected in the growing number of college programs on the subject. Entrepreneurship majors and minors were almost unheard of 15 years ago; now, enough exist for the Princeton Review to rank the top 50.[55]

This resurgence of interest in entrepreneurship is good news for the economy, as new firms are potent job creators. Businesses less than a year old create an average of 3 million jobs each year, and contribute to job growth even during recessions.[56] Those less than five years old created 40 million jobs in the past 25 years, or 20% of total gross and net job growth.[57] High-growth firms, sometimes called "gazelles" for their leaping trajectories, add an average of 88 employees per year, compared to the two to three employees added by low-growth firms. Such firms tend to be newer: 76% of them are less than five years old.[58] Though they represent less than 1% of all businesses, gazelle firms are found in all industries, from the Silicon Valley startups of recent renown to businesses specializing in construction, social services, energy, and utilities.[59]

Franchises

Some people would like to be their own bosses, but don't want to incur the risk of starting their own companies from scratch. For such individuals, buying a franchise can be an ideal career move.

Franchises are a small but highly visible subset of American businesses. There are over 450,000 franchised establishments in the United States, over 350,000 of which are owned by franchisees, and they employ 7.8 million people.[60] Though they contribute only 3% of US GDP, franchises account for 40% of retail sales.[61] About 44% of the 3,000 franchised brands in the United States are in the accommodation and food services sector, while 28% are retailers and 7% are real estate, rental, and leasing companies.[62]

To the right kind of person, owning a franchise can be a better choice than starting an independent business. For one thing, franchises are established brands with business models that have proven successful. Franchisors also provide franchisees with training, ongoing support, and assistance with such aspects of business ownership as marketing and acquiring real estate. They can use their clout and larger scale to help franchisees negotiate for lower prices on furniture, uniforms, inventory, and other essential supplies.[63]

Generally speaking, owning a franchise is less risky than starting your own business, though the success of any store hinges on the skill of its operator. Individual franchise brands have widely varying success rates, and potential franchisees need to do their research and select a franchise with care. (A couple of good places to start are the Small Business Administration, which regularly publishes a list of the franchises with the highest loan failure rates, and *Entrepreneur* magazine, which ranks the top 500 franchises in the country on a yearly basis.) Rather than choosing a franchise because it's trendy, buyers should find one that matches their skills, budget, and tolerance for risk.[64]

Franchising experts caution that franchises are not "businesses in a box" or "turnkey operations" that run themselves. Buying one can cost you hundreds of thousands of dollars up front, plus ongoing royalty fees. If your operation fails, you could end up owing plenty of money to a franchisor or landlord. Franchises are also not good options for independent-minded people who will bristle at having to follow procedures set by someone else or answer to corporate headquarters. But, for the right individual, owning a franchise can be a rewarding path to self-employment.[65]

Small Businesses

Small businesses, defined by the Small Business Administration as companies that are independently owned and operated, designed to make a profit, and not dominant in their field, are vital to the US economy.[66] They generate more than $6 trillion in revenue and produce over half the nation's nonfarm GDP.[67]

Small businesses are also crucial to the workforce. Over 99% of all employer firms are small businesses.[68] More potent job creators than large firms, small businesses have provided 55% of all jobs, created 66% of all new jobs, and been responsible for 54% of all sales since the 1970s.[69] They have provided 11.8 million of the 18.5 million net new jobs created between 1993 and 2011.[70]

In many ways, small businesses are more innovative than larger companies. Out of high-patenting firms, for example, small companies produce 16 times more patents than large ones.[71] Small businesses' size often makes it easier for them to respond to changing market conditions, and they frequently have to be creative in their use of their more limited resources.[72]

Medium-Sized Firms

Though the media prefers to focus on large corporations and small businesses, medium-sized firms are just as essential to the economy. Middle-market firms—companies with revenues between $10 million and $1 billion—employ over 40 million Americans.[73] They are responsible for around one-third of the US private sector's GDP and reap over $9 trillion in annual revenue.[74] If the US middle market was its own economy, it would be the fourth largest in the world, just behind Japan's and ahead of Germany's.[75]

There are about 197,000 middle-market firms in the United States, many of them located in the country's industrial heartland.[76] These firms tend to be long-lived. Their average age is 31 years,[77] and almost 70% have been in business over 20 years. They are far more likely than large firms to rely upon local and regional suppliers, and are often considered pillars of their communities.[78]

Medium-sized firms also tend to be stable, even in tough economic times. During the recession years of 2007–2010, medium-sized firms added 2.2 million jobs, while large firms lost 3.7 million. In 2010–2011, they increased their employment by 3.8%, whereas big firms increased theirs by only .8% and small firms by 2.5%. Eighty-two percent of companies in the middle market survived the recession, compared to only 57% of small firms.[79]

Middle-market companies' smaller size can render them more nimble than larger firms. They often find it easier to innovate, switch direction, and adapt to changing conditions.[80] The National Center for the Middle Market finds they are more focused on what their customers want than their larger counterparts, and that they use more cutting-edge management methods.[81] And technologies such as cloud computing, software-as-a-service, and social media have made it easier for medium-sized firms to cut costs and compete with larger firms.[82]

This propensity for innovation allows medium-sized firms to grow. Twenty-seven percent of all large companies in 2010 were medium-sized in 2005. Eighty percent of middle-market firms anticipate adding growth in the next year.[83]

Nonprofits

The nonprofit sector appeals to people looking to make a difference. Though it typically pays less—in some cases, far less—than the private sector,[84] the nonprofit sector offers employees more in terms of intangible rewards like the ability to give back to their communities and contribute to causes they care about.

Broader than many people realize, the nonprofit sector encompasses not only charities and foundations but many other types of institutions. Technically, the term *nonprofit* refers to any nonbusiness or nongovernmental organization that is exempt from income tax. Many hospitals, museums, nursing homes, advocacy groups, colleges and universities, and religious, scientific, and literary organizations are considered nonprofits, and nonprofits employ members of almost every profession.[85]

The nonprofit sector is a growing field offering plentiful opportunities for advancement. Between 1994 and 2007, the sector grew 50% larger, from 1.1 million organizations employing 5.4 million people to 1.64 million employing 8.7 million.[86] Nonprofit job growth increased 2.1% annually from 2000 to 2010, even as the private sector lost net jobs, partly because many nonprofit organizations belong to the growing healthcare and education industries.[87]

Due to this growth and the impending retirement of the Baby Boomers, nonprofits will face a serious leadership gap in the near future. Sixty-five percent of nonprofits anticipate leadership turnover in the next five years, and 55% of executive directors at nonprofits are over 50.[88] In 2008, an estimated 24,000 nonprofit leadership positions were left vacant,[89] while, by 2016, nonprofits are projected to have 80,000 unfilled openings for senior leaders.[90] These vacancies translate to ample opportunity for service-minded individuals.

Public Sector Jobs

Though today's employment landscape is marked by churn and change, many people still want secure, long-lasting jobs that provide good benefits. If you're one of them, you may want to consider working in the public sector. The US government provides millions of stable jobs with excellent health and retirement benefits, and employs workers of all skill and experience levels across a wide variety of positions, from web developers to HR managers, administrative assistants, and engineers.

Over 10 million American civilians are employed by the government, 2.3 million of them by the federal government[91] and the rest by state and local governments. Around 70% of federal employees are local, including firefighters, police, and teachers in public schools.[92]

Although Capitol Hill is the first thing many of us think of when we hear "government," only 15% of government positions are based in Washington. There are public sector jobs available in all 50 states, and 50,000 of them are headquartered overseas.[93]

Stability is a key reason people seek government jobs. Though the government may shed jobs due to budget cuts, it won't go out of business. Plus, some jobs offer tenure, which make it difficult for workers to be fired.[94] The government also provides solid benefits: government employees are typically eligible for better-quality health insurance at lower cost than private sector employees. And some 79% of government employees receive pensions.[95]

Also, many government positions will open up over the next few years as Baby Boomers retire, creating opportunities for employees of private companies to switch sectors. About 25% of federal employees will soon reach retirement age.[96]

The public sector may not be the best option for those looking for a fast-paced work environment, however. As a bureaucracy the government can be, well, bureaucratic: slow to change, procedure-bound, and mired in red tape. Salary growth is often slower in the public sector, which provides fewer opportunities for merit-based raises.[97]

Whether the government pays better than private employers is a matter for debate. According to the Bureau of Labor Statistics, public sector employees are paid 5% more, across the board, than those in the private sector, but this varies significantly by position. Accountants and executives, to give just two examples, are typically paid better by private employers than they are by the government.[98]

If you're curious about public sector jobs, learn about the different agencies and departments to see which might be the best fit for you. The Partnership for Public Service publishes a yearly ranking of the best places to work in the federal government, available at bestplacestowork.org. Most government job openings are posted on USAjobs.gov, but some openings will only be listed on individual agencies' websites, so periodically check the ones you're interested in.

You'll need a more detailed resume called a federal resume to apply for government jobs.[99] To learn about the requirements for a federal resume, visit gogovernment.org. Agencies do have their own jargon, so you may need to learn some of the terminology used by the agencies you're targeting to have the right keywords on your resume.[100]

Inside the Corporation

When planning your career, it's important to take into account the culture of the companies you plan to work for. In some cases, a firm's culture may have a larger impact on how satisfied you are working there than its size or location. Many people choose alternatives to working for a large corporation, such as freelancing, entrepreneurship, or working for a small or medium-sized firm, because they believe corporations won't provide them with enough flexibility or autonomy. But that's not always the case. Some innovative large companies now offer employees flexible working or scheduling arrangements, while others prioritize employee empowerment by allowing for democratic decision making and project-based work. These companies are a viable alternative to self-employment for individuals seeking greater control over their schedules and the projects they work on.

Some forward-thinking companies have made provisions for employees to have flexible career paths *without* seeking employment elsewhere. Deloitte, for instance, pioneered Mass Career Customization, a program which allows employees to adjust the pace, intensity, location, schedule, and responsibility level of their workload at different points in their career.[101] Deloitte has found that workers are more loyal when they feel supported, especially during the crucial phase of family formation, and more likely to remain with the company.[102]

For decades, most jobs have been measured by "face time": the amount of hours an employee puts in at a certain place. Now, due to mobile technology that makes it possible for knowledge workers to work from nearly anywhere, the phrase "nine-to-five" is beginning to sound a little quaint. Starting in the 1990s, companies began to implement flexible working policies, such as compressed workweeks, variable arrival and departure times, reduced hours, bankable hours, and job sharing, that freed employees from time constraints (see Figure 2.2).[103] Now, thanks to the rise of high-speed wireless Internet, organizations have become more accommodating about *where* employees work as well.

Telecommuting has seen rapid growth over the past decade. Estimates of the number of telecommuters vary widely, depending on whether self-employed people are defined as teleworkers, but around 33.7 million people now work from home at least once a month, and 2.9 million primarily work from home. In 2010, 34% of employers offered at least some telecommuting options, up from 26% in 2006.[104] Employees of all levels work remotely, and 40% of teleworkers hold leadership positions.[105] Some corporations have implemented versions of

Flexibility Improves In Some Areas . . .
Percentage of employers allowing at least some employees to:

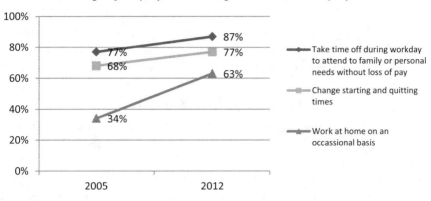

. . . But Not Others
Percentage of employers allowing at least some employees to:

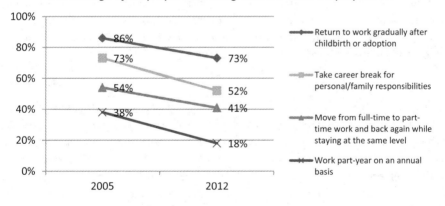

Figure 2.2. Source: Kenneth Matos and Ellen Galinsky, *2012 National Study of Employers* (New York: Families and Work Institute, 2012), 16–17, http://familiesandwork.org/site/research/reports/NSE_2012.pdf.

telecommuting known as results-only work environments, or ROWEs, in which employees are paid solely for what they do, not when or where they do it.

Flexible work arrangements have proven benefits for both workers and their employers. Employees using them often experience higher job satisfaction, less stress, and more time with their families, and are less likely to leave their jobs.[106]

After Xerox introduced a policy allowing anyone, regardless of family status, to use flextime, absenteeism dropped by 30%, employees reported feeling more empowered, and supervisors felt less need to micromanage.[107] Telecommuting initiatives have also saved companies money and made them more environmentally friendly. By letting most of its 45,000 employees work from home, Deloitte reduced its office space and energy costs by 30%, saving $30 million in 2008 alone after redesigning offices for telecommuters who did not need permanent desks.[108]

Changing Workplaces

Once, most companies' organizational charts resembled pyramids: fixed structures with clear upward trajectories. Today, the best metaphor for the organization of many companies is the network: fluid, connected, agile, and ever-changing. Employees of such firms are both literally and figuratively networked. They're linked to vast amounts of information, to one another, and to stakeholders through high-speed Internet, and they behave like the parts of a network, arranging themselves into temporary project teams that come together or disband as circumstances change. In networked corporations, workers tend to be entrusted with more freedom. Within certain parameters, they may choose whether to work at home or at the office, which hours they work, what projects they work on, and which colleagues they work with. But they're also required to be more responsible and self-directed, managing their time and relationships carefully and taking charge of their own learning and career paths.

Project-Based Work

Picture a Hollywood or indie film. Actors, writers, directors, cinematographers, editors, costume designers, and myriad other professionals sign on to film projects which interest them, or which they think will advance their careers. They work together as a team until the film is completed, at which point they are free to join other projects, perhaps working for different studios, with different sets of people.[109] In many of America's most innovative corporations, including Google, Facebook, Microsoft, Apple, and Hewlett-Packard, work is performed in a similar fashion.[110] Employees work on temporary project-based teams, the membership of which is always shifting. Innovations such as the iPhone and Google's driverless car were developed by such teams.[111]

Some companies have implemented internal labor markets in which employees use social media to build their own project teams or promote their credentials to increase the likelihood they'll be chosen for projects that intrigue them.[112] Hewlett-Packard, for instance, operates an internal crowdsourcing initiative called the VC Café that enables employees to submit project proposals to senior management. Approved projects receive funding and are posted internally so interested colleagues can apply to work on them.[113]

Project-based work often benefits both employees and organizations. When people have greater control over what they work on and who they work with, they tend to be more satisfied with their jobs, more dedicated to their employers, and more creative. Having the freedom to work in different areas of a company also broadens their skill sets and networks, making them more valuable and well-rounded employees. And, when anyone, regardless of rank, is empowered to put forth ideas, innovation can spring from unexpected places.[114]

Flat Hierarchies

Project-based work, or, indeed, any work that involves a high degree of teamwork and collaboration, all but demands fluid management styles and structures. Companies have found that strict hierarchies and fixed chains of command are not conducive to innovation. When employees feel they are being given marching orders from higher-ups who may not be experts in their subject area or hold their depth of expertise, they can feel stifled, restricted, and less willing to share their knowledge and ideas. But when employees are encouraged to speak up, empowered to make decisions about issues that affect them, and managed by individuals who act as coaches or facilitators rather than enforcers, they tend to be more satisfied, committed, and creative.[115]

Realizing that flatter organizational structures can promote innovation, many companies have taken steps to give employees greater control over their work, and even over major organizational changes.[116] At Gore-Tex maker W.L. Gore, for instance, teams of workers are authorized to implement multimillion-dollar decisions such as whether to develop new types of manufacturing equipment.[117] Facebook hosts an internal creative commons in which all employees are invited to have a say on the direction the company is taking.[118] At Cisco, many decisions are made by ad-hoc councils composed of employees who represent different business functions, product lines, and operating regions. This structure has helped improve the company's bottom line. One employee council voted to shift $100 million and 500 employees to the small business market. In just one fiscal year, this decision expanded Cisco's small business portfolio by 100 new products, a rate of change that would have been unlikely under a more hierarchical system.[119]

Some avant-garde companies take flatness to new extremes. At videogame maker Valve, which describes itself as "boss-free," there are no managers and no promotions, hiring decisions are made by teams, and salaries are determined by staff vote.[120]

Flat organizational structures have their advantages. Members of younger generations tend to enjoy the mix of informality and empowerment they provide, and 78% of executives agree they help attract prospective employees.[121] But flat structures do require that employees adopt new, and perhaps unfamiliar, mindsets and skill sets. Leaders in flat organizations will need to act as coordinators rather than controllers, sharing power, generating enthusiasm for projects, and eliciting information and ideas from people at all levels of their organizations. Employees of flat companies must be self-disciplined and motivated, market their assets and project ideas to colleagues, and strategically choose projects that align well with their career goals.

Changing Needs

If one word could encapsulate all the trends discussed in this chapter, it would be "autonomy." Technology has empowered workers, both inside and outside the corporation, to take greater control over their schedules and the content of their work. Flexible work arrangements, project-based teams, and flat hierarchies all point to a movement towards greater employee autonomy within the corporation, while freelancers, entrepreneurs, and small business owners have chosen career paths that free them from the confines of traditional employment.

Most employees enjoy having more control over how, when, and where they work, and find that such freedom makes them happier, more creative, and more satisfied with their jobs. But, to thrive under these more flexible working conditions, you must take charge of your career, in effect acting as your own boss. Some core skills you'll need to succeed in a more fluid workplace include:

- *Strategic thinking about career paths.* In companies with flatter hierarchies and those that rely on project teams, employees' reputations and skill sets can be more meaningful than their job titles. Yet workers in these more egalitarian environments still need to be strategic about their career goals—perhaps even more so than in firms with linear pathways to advancement. Whether you are motivated by money, prestige, novelty, or the opportunity to work on more interesting projects, you'll need to set objectives, map out the skills you have and those you need to cultivate, connect with the right people, and choose the work opportunities that best further your goals. (In Chapter 7, we'll provide you with a framework you can use to start planning your strategy.) You should also be able to describe the value of your contributions in concrete ways that go beyond job titles, such as metrics, media hits, or money earned or saved for your employers.[122]

  Again, cultivating an entrepreneurial mindset is essential, whether you work for a corporation or for yourself. You need to be able to market yourself and your skills, craft a strong personal brand, carefully manage your online reputation, and get others excited about your ideas. Freelancers who consider themselves entrepreneurs, surveys show, are more satisfied with their careers and have higher hourly rates than those who don't.[123] Not thinking in business terms, conversely, can hurt freelancers.

Fifty-three percent of freelancers spend less than five hours per month on self-promotion, even though this essential activity can improve their earnings.[124]

- *Social media savvy.* Social media is "the next Office suite," according to HootSuite CEO Ryan Holmes: a basic business skill almost everyone will be expected to have.[125] Seventy-nine percent of companies now use or plan to use social media,[126] and most freelancers and small business owners consider social networks an essential part of their marketing strategies. Learn to make the most of social media: Choose the platforms that best meet your needs, build connections, join groups, answer questions, share knowledge, and create a compelling and friendly online persona.

- *Networking.* Personal connections have always greased the wheels of business, and, today, they may be more important than ever. The Internet has increased competition for work: Employers' inboxes are flooded with resumes, while freelancers find themselves competing with thousands of other contractors on oDesk and Elance. Being well-connected can help you stand out in such a crowded market. Networking, whether face-to-face or virtual, can introduce you to leads on new projects or gigs: 68% of freelancers find clients through referrals, word-of-mouth, or tapping their networks.[127]

- *In-person and virtual team building.* In networked corporations, as well as on freelancing job sites like oDesk, employees' reputations rely on how well they work with teams. Wherever you work, you'll need to be an excellent communicator and rapport builder who practices good social skills such as self-management, negotiation, conflict management, giving feedback, and etiquette.[128] As you'll likely work on an interdisciplinary team at some point, strive for a T-shaped skill set: deep experience in one subject area coupled with broad knowledge of related areas. In particular, cultivate a general understanding of your teammates' areas of expertise to better understand the terminology, principles, and logic they use.[129]

- *Leadership through cultivation and connection.* In networked corporations, the most effective leaders will act less like managers and more like facilitators. They'll act as points of connection between project teams and organizations, serving as channels through which information flows, solving problems, breaking down silos, and preventing bottlenecks.[130] Such leaders will understand what motivates their followers, and shape their team's work to fit their company's goals. They will coordinate value networks, and create inclusive cultures in which innovation flourishes.[131]

Notes

1. Kathy Robertson, "How Long Do Workers Stay in Jobs?" *Sacramento Business Journal*, December 27, 2012, http://www.bizjournals.com/sacramento/news/2012/12/27/how-long-do-americans-stay-in-jobs.html?page=all.

2. Organizational psychologist Elliot Jaques coined the term in his classic 1965 article "Death and the Midlife Crisis."

3. Cisco, *Transitioning to Workforce 2020* (San Jose: Cisco, 2011), 13, http://www.cisco.com/web/learning/employer_resources/pdfs/Workforce_2020_White_Paper.pdf.

4. Towers Watson, *The New Employment Deal: How Far, How Fast and How Enduring? Insights from the 2010 Global Workforce Study* (New York: Towers Watson, 2010), 7, unav.es%2Ficf%2Fmain%2Ftop%2F2010%2FTowers_Global-Workfoce-Study-2010.pdf&ei=afEgUq-uNPOosAStoIGgCw&usg=AFQjCNHRBw0zloccH56BUZBKTOJZx9yNdg&sig2=PQMjlTefsesKwyW0prjdnQ&bvm=bv.51495398,d.cWc.

5. Cisco, *Transitioning to Workforce 2020*, 17.

6. Towers Watson, *New Employment Deal*, 15.

7. Alison Maitland and Peter Thomson, *Future Work: How Businesses Can Adapt and Thrive in the New World of Work* (Basingstoke, UK: Palgrave Macmillan, 2011), 21.

8. Towers Watson, *New Employment Deal*, 11.

9. Cisco, *Transitioning to Workforce 2020*, 17.

10. Ibid., 18.

11. A further 22% are "unsupported": They care about their companies and jobs, but don't feel they have the tools and support they need to perform to the best of their ability. Towers Watson, *2012 Global Workforce Study. Engagement at Risk: Driving Strong Performance in a Volatile Global Environment* (New York: Towers Watson, 2012), 6, http://www.towerswatson.com/en/Insights/IC-Types/Survey-Research-Results/2012/07/2012-Towers-Watson-Global-Workforce-Study.

12. Ibid., 5.

13. Wharton School of the University of Pennsylvania, "Declining Employee Loyalty: A Casualty of the New Workplace," *Knowledge@Wharton*, May 9, 2012, http://knowledge.wharton.upenn.edu/article.cfm?articleid=2995.

14. Towers Watson, *New Employment Deal*, 7.

15. Lynda Gratton, *The Shift: The Future of Work Is Already Here* (London: HarperCollins, 2011), 163.

16. Deborah O'Neil and Diana Bilimoria, "Women's Career Development Phases: Idealism, Endurance, and Reinvention," *Career Development International* 10, no. 3 (2005): 181.

17. Gratton, *Shift*, 168.

18. Lisa A. Mainiero and Sherry E. Sullivan, "Kaleidoscope Careers: An Alternate Explanation for the 'Opt-Out' Revolution," *Academy of Management Executive* 19, no. 1 (2005): 111, 113; O'Neil and Bilimoria, "Women's Career Development Phases"; Deborah O'Neil, Margaret M. Hopkins, and Diana Bilimoria, "Women's Careers at the Start of the 21st Century: Patterns and Paradoxes," *Journal of Business Ethics* 80 (2008): 731, doi:10.1007/s10551-007-9465-6.

19. O'Neil and Bilimoria, "Women's Career Development Phases," 181.

20. Lisa A. Mainiero and Sherry E. Sullivan, *The Opt-Out Revolt: Why People Are Leaving Companies to Create Kaleidoscope Careers* (Mountain View, CA: Davies-Black, 2006), 212.

21. Ibid., 89.

22. Ibid., 212.

23. Gratton, *Shift*, 251.

24. Mainiero and Sullivan, *Opt-Out Revolt*, 8-9.

25. Mainiero and Sullivan, "Kaleidoscope," 112–13.

26. Sylvia Ann Hewlett and Carolyn Buck Luce, "Off-Ramps and On-Ramps: Keeping Talented Women on the Road to Success," *Harvard Business Review*, March 2005, 5, http://hbr.org/2005/03/off-ramps-and-on-ramps-keeping-talented-women-on-the-road-to-success/ar/1.

27. Betsy Morris and Ruth M. Coxeter, "Executive Women Confront Midlife Crisis," *Fortune*, September 18, 1995, http://money.cnn.com/magazines/fortune/fortune_archive/1995/09/18/206085/index.htm.

28. Gary N. Powell and Lisa A. Mainiero, "Cross-Currents in the River of Time: Conceptualizing the Complexities of Women's Careers," *Journal of Management* 18, no. 2 (1992): 223; Mainiero and Sullivan, "Kaleidoscope," 110, 113.

29. Mainiero and Sullivan, *Opt-Out Revolt*, 309.

30. Elizabeth F. Cabrera, "Opting Out and Opting In: Understanding the Complexities of Women's Career Transitions," *Career Development International* 12, no. 3 (2007): 1, http://e-archivo.uc3m.es/bitstream/10016/11270/1/opting_cabrera_CDI_2007_ps.pdf.

31. Mainiero and Sullivan, *Opt-Out Revolt*, 38.

32. Ibid., 310.

33. Ibid., 121, 132, 148.

34. Ibid., 136, 148.

35. Maitland and Thomson, *Future Work*, 29.

36. Derek Thompson, "The Future of America Is Freelance," *The Atlantic*, September 17, 2010, http://www.theatlantic.com/business/archive/2010/09/the-future-of-america-is-freelance/63171/.

37. Tracey Wilen-Daugenti, *Society 3.0: How Technology Is Reshaping Education, Work and Society* (New York: Peter Lang, 2012), 83.

38. Elance, "Freelance Talent Report," June 2011, https://www.elance.com/q/freelance-talent-report-2011.

39. Ed Gandia, *2012 Freelance Industry Report* (Marietta, GA: International Freelancers Academy; Richland, GA: Back of the House, 2012), 12, https://s3.amazonaws.com/ifdconference/2012report/Freelance+Industry+Report+2012+updated.pdf.

40. Ibid.

41. Ibid., 14–15, 17–18.

42. Fabio Rosati, "A Business of One: 5 Strategies for Successful Freelancing," *CIO Network* (blog), *Forbes*, June 4, 2012, http://www.forbes.com/sites/ciocentral/2012/06/04/a-business-of-one-5-strategies-for-successful-freelancing/.

43. Paul Davidson, "Freelance Workers Reshape Companies and Jobs," *USA Today*, October 13, 2010, http://usatoday30.usatoday.com/money/economy/employment/2010-10-13-1Acontractworkers13_CV_N.htm.

44. Rebecca Callahan, "Blended Workforce: The New Norm," *Talent Management*, September 9, 2011, http://talentmgt.com/articles/view/blended-workforce-the-new-norm/print:1.

45. Deloitte, *The 2011 Shift Index: Measuring the Forces of Long-Term Change* (New York: Deloitte, 2011), 12, http://www.deloitte.com/assets/dcom-unitedstates/local%20assets/documents/us_tmt_2011shiftindex_111011.pdf.

46. Elance, "Global Small Business Survey Uncovers Online Workforce Is the New Face of Economic Recovery," news release, June 13, 2012, https://www.elance.com/q/node/1352.

47. Ibid.

48. Thompson, "Future of America Is Freelance."

49. Gandia, *2012 Freelance Industry Report*, 20.

50. Davidson, "Freelance Workers Reshape Companies."

51. Karen E. Klein, "Are Entrepreneurs Born or Made?," *Businessweek*, July 23, 2010, http://www.businessweek.com/smallbiz/content/jul2010/sb20100723_154719.htm.

52. Donna J. Kelley, et al., *Global Entrepreneurship Monitor. United States Report 2011* (London: Global Entrepreneurship Research Association, 2011), 7, http://www.gemconsortium.org/docs/2618/gem-unied-states-2011-report.

53. Rebecca Walker, "Gen Y Grads More Likely to Launch Start-Ups," *USA Today*, May 8, 2010, http://usatoday30.usatoday.com/money/smallbusiness/story/2012-05-07/generation-y-entrepreneurs-small-business/54814472/1.

54. Ewing Marion Kauffman Foundation, "An Entrepreneurial Generation of 18- to 34-Year-Olds Wants to Start Companies When Economy Rebounds, According to New Poll," news release, November 10, 2011, http://www.kauffman.org/newsroom/millennials-want-to-start-companies-when-economy-rebounds-poll-says.aspx.

55. Michelle Juergen, "The Top 50 Entrepreneurship Programs," *Entrepreneur*, October 2011, http://www.entrepreneur.com/article/220327.

56. Tim Kane, *The Importance of Startups in Job Creation and Job Destruction* (Kansas City, MO: Ewing Marion Kauffman Foundation, 2010), 2, http://www.kauffman.org/uploadedfiles/firm_formation_importance_of_startups.pdf.

57. John Horn and Darren Pleasance, "Restarting the US Small-Business Growth Engine," *McKinsey Quarterly*, November 2012, https://www.mckinseyquarterly.com/Restarting_the_US_small_business_growth_engine_3032.

58. Ibid.

59. Ibid.

60. US Census Bureau, *2007 Economic Census: Franchise Statistics* (Washington, DC: US Census Bureau, 2007), 1, http://www.census.gov/econ/census/pdf/franchise_flyer.pdf.

61. "Small Business Trends," US Small Business Administration, accessed August 8, 2013, http://www.sba.gov/content/small-business-trends.

62. US Census Bureau, *Franchise Statistics*, 2.

63. Jeff Elgin, "Top 10 Reasons to Buy a Franchise," *Entrepreneur*, December 27, 2007, http://www.entrepreneur.com/article/188452; Geoff Williams, "Reasons You Should Buy a Franchise (And Reasons You Shouldn't)," *US News and World Report*, February 27, 2013, http://money.usnews.com/money/personal-finance/articles/2013/02/27/reasons-you-should-buy-a-franchise-and-reasons-you-shouldnt.

64. Joel Libava, "Franchise Failure Rate: Myths and Facts," *American Express Open Forum*, December 9, 2008, https://www.openforum.com/articles/franchise-failure-rate-myths-and-facts-1/.

65. Williams, "Reasons You Should Buy a Franchise."

66. "What Is SBA's Definition of a Small Business Concern?" US Small Business Administration, accessed February 1, 2012, http://www.sba.gov/content/what-sbas-definition-small-business-concern.

67. Steve King and Carolyn Ockels, *Intuit Future of Small Business Report. Research Brief: Defining Small Business Innovation* (Mountain View, CA: Intuit, 2009), 1, http://http-download.intuit.com/http.intuit/CMO/intuit/futureofsmallbusiness/intuit_fosb_report_march_2009.pdf.

68. US Small Business Administration, *Frequently Asked Questions* (Washington, DC: US Small Business Administration, 2012), 1, http://www.sba.gov/sites/default/files/FAQ_Sept_2012.pdf.

69. "Small Business Trends," US Small Business Administration.

70. US Small Business Administration, *Frequently Asked Questions*, 1.

71. Ibid., 3.

72. King and Ockels, *Intuit Future of Small Business Report*, 1, 3.

73. "The Mighty Middle," *The Economist*, October 20, 2012, http://www.economist.com/news/business/21564893-medium-sized-firms-are-unsung-heroes-america%E2%80%99s-economy.

74. Ohio State University and General Electric Capital, *The Market That Moves America: Insights, Perspectives, and Opportunities from Middle Market Companies* (Columbus, OH: The Ohio State University; Norwalk, CT: General Electric Capital, 2011), 1, 4, http://www.middlemarketcenter.org/stuff/contentmgr/files/0/5a30759c139d09a882c7083f0f00d299/download/the_market_that_moves_america_white_paper.pdf.

75. Ibid., 7.

76. "The Mighty Middle," *Economist*.

77. Ibid.

78. Ohio State University and General Electric Capital, *The Market That Moves America*, 4, 8.

79. "The Mighty Middle," *Economist*.

80. Dave Maney, "Why the Middle Market Matters—Now More Than Ever," *CNBC*, September 26, 2011, http://www.cnbc.com/id/44639661.

81. "The Mighty Middle," *Economist*.

82. Maney, "Why The Middle Market Matters."

83. Ohio State University and General Electric Capital, *The Market That Moves America*, 4, 9.

84. Rachel Zupek, "Maximizing a Non-Profit Salary," *CNN*, May 16, 2007, http://www.cnn.com/2007/US/Careers/05/16/cb.profit/.

85. Lester M. Salamon, S. Wojciech Sokolowski, and Stephanie L. Geller, *Nonprofit Employment Bulletin No. 39, Holding the Fort: Nonprofit Employment During a Decade of Turmoil* (Baltimore: Johns Hopkins University Center for Civil Society Studies, 2012), 1, http://ccss.jhu.edu/wp-content/uploads/downloads/2012/01/NED_National_2012.pdf; White House Project, *The White House Project: Benchmarking Women's Leadership* (New York: The White House Project, 2009), 75, http://www.in.gov/icw/files/benchmark_wom_leadership.pdf.

86. White House Project, *Benchmarking Women's Leadership*, 75.

87. Salamon, Sokolowski, and Geller, *Holding the Fort*, 3, 5.

88. R. Patrick Halpern, *Workforce Issues in the Nonprofit Sector* (Kansas City, MO: American Humanics Initiative for Nonprofit Sector Careers, .2006), 5, http://www.nassembly.org/Collaborations/PeerNetworks/documents/AmericanHumanicsWorkforceLiteratureReviewandBibliography4-26-06.pdf.

89. David Simms and Carol Trager, *Finding Leaders for America's Nonprofits* (New York: The Bridgespan Group, 2009), 1, http://www.bridgespan.org/WorkArea/linkit.aspx?LinkIdentifier=id&ItemID=3824.

90. Nonprofit Leadership Alliance, *The Skills the Nonprofit Sector Requires of Its Managers and Leaders* (Kansas City, MO: Nonprofit Leadership Alliance, 2011), 2, http://www.nonprofitleadershipalliance.org/cnp/cnprevalidation/Final%20Report.pdf.

91. Nancy Collamer, "5 Tips for Getting a Government Job," *Forbes*, November 14, 2012, http://www.forbes.com/sites/nextavenue/2012/11/14/5-tips-for-getting-a-government-job/.

92. James Mannion, "A Wealth of Opportunities," *Netplaces*, accessed August 8, 2012, http://www.netplaces.com/government-jobs/so-you-want-to-work-for-the-government/a-wealth-of-opportunities.htm.

93. Courtney Rubin, "How to Make a Career in Public Service," *US News and World Report*, October 28, 2010, http://www.usnews.com/news/articles/2010/10/28/how-to-make-a-career-in-public-service.

94. James Mannion, "Top 10 Reasons to Consider a Government Job," *Netplaces*, accessed August 11, 2013, http://www.netplaces.com/government-jobs/so-you-want-to-work-for-the-government/top-ten-reasons-to-consider-a-government-job.htm.

95. Michael James, "Working in America: Public vs. Private Sector," *ABC News*, February 18, 2011, http://abcnews.go.com/blogs/politics/2011/02/working-in-america-public-vs-private-sector/.

96. Collamer, "5 Tips."

97. Michael Roberts, "The Pros and Cons of a Government Job," *About.com*, accessed August 11, 2013, http://govcareers.about.com/od/StartingOut/a/The-Pros-And-Cons-Of-A-Government-Job.

98. James, "Public vs. Private Sector."

99. "Frequently Asked Questions," *Go Government*, accessed August 11, 2013, http://gogovernment.org/about/faqs.php.

100. Collamer, "5 Tips."

101. Cathleen Benko and Anne Weisberg, *Mass Career Customization: Aligning the Workplace with Today's Nontraditional Workforce* (Cambridge, MA: Harvard Business School, 2007), 15.

102. Ibid., 7.

103. Ibid., 58; Maitland and Thomson, *Future Work*, 29.

104. Dori Meinert, "Make Telecommuting Pay Off," *HR Magazine* 56 (2011): 34.

105. Michael O'Neill, *Future Work and Work Trends* (East Greenville, PA: Knoll Workplace Research, 2009), 2, http://www.knoll.com/research/downloads/WP_future_work_work_trends.pdf.

106. Laurel A. McNall, Aline D. Masuda, and Jessica M. Nicklin, "Flexible Work Arrangements, Job Satisfaction, and Turnover Intentions: The Mediating Role of Work-to-Family Enrichment," *The Journal of Psychology* 144 (2010): 61; Lotte Bailyn, "Redesigning Work for Gender Equity and Work-Personal Life Integration," *Community, Work & Family* 14 (2011), 102.

107. Bailyn, "Redesigning Work," 101–2.

108. Meinert, "Make Telecommuting Pay," 34.

109. Institute for the Future for Apollo Research Institute, *The Future of Work* (Palo Alto: Institute for the Future; Phoenix, AZ: Apollo Research Institute, 2012), 3, http://apolloresearchinstitute.com/research-studies/workforce-preparedness/future-work (site discontinued).

110. Eric Matson, "Project: You," *Fast Company*, December 31, 1997, http://www.fastcompany.com/33738/project-you; "Work at Google," Google, accessed July 1, 2013, http://research.google.com/workatgoogle.html.

111. Ina Fried, "Apple's Scott Forstall on How 'Project Purple' Became the iPhone," *All Things D*, August 3, 2012, http://allthingsd.com/20120803/apples-scott-forstall-on-how-project-purple-turned-into-the-iphone/.

112. Thomas W. Malone, *The Future of Work: How the New Order of Business Will Shape Your Organization, Your Management Style, and Your Life* (Cambridge, MA: Harvard Business School Press, 2004), 92–93.

113. Ibid., 93.

114. David Bollier, *The Future of Work: What It Means for Individuals, Businesses, Markets and Governments* (Washington, DC: The Aspen Institute, 2011), 18, 20, http://www.aspeninstitute.org/sites/default/files/content/docs/pubs/The_Future_of_Work.pdf; Malone, *Future of Work*, 34–35.

115. Malone, *Future of Work*, 34.

116. Cisco, *Transitioning to Workforce 2020*, 22.

117. Rachel Emma Silverman, "Who's the Boss? There Isn't One," *Wall Street Journal*, June 19, 2012, http://online.wsj.com/article/SB10001424052702303379204577474953586383604.html.

118. Institute for the Future for Apollo Research Institute, *The Future of Work*, 2.

119. Cisco, *Transitioning to Workforce 2020*, 23–4.

120. Silverman, "Who's the Boss?"

121. Cisco, *Transitioning to Workforce 2020*, 25.

122. Matson, "Project: You."

123. Gandia, *2012 Freelance Industry Report*, 62.

124. Ibid, 53.

125. Ryan Holmes, "The Can't-Miss Social Media Trends for 2013," *Fast Company*, November 29, 2012, http://www.fastcompany.com/3003473/cant-miss-social-media-trends-2013.

126. Ryan Holmes, "5 Ways Social Media Will Change the Way You Work in 2013," *CIO Network* (blog), *Forbes*, December 11, 2012, http://www.forbes.com/sites/ciocentral/2012/12/11/5-ways-social-media-will-change-the-way-you-work-in-2013/.

127. Gandia, *2012 Freelance Industry Report,* 20.

128. Institute for the Future for Apollo Research Institute, *Future Work Skills 2020* (Palo Alto, CA: Institute for the Future; Phoenix, AZ: Apollo Research Institute, 2011), 12, http://www.iftf.org/uploads/media/SR-1382A_UPRI_future_work_skills_sm.pdf; Bollier, *Future of Work,* 8.

129. Institute for the Future for Apollo Research Institute, *Future Work Skills 2020,* 11; Bollier, *Future of Work,* 8.

130. Cisco, *Transitioning to Workforce 2020,* 28.

131. Institute for the Future for Apollo Research Institute, *Future of Work Report: Flat-World Labor* (Palo Alto, CA: Institute for the Future; Phoenix, AZ: Apollo Research Institute, 2012), 2, http://apolloresearchinstitute.com/sites/default/files/future-of-work-report-flat-world-labor.pdf (site discontinued); Cisco, *Transitioning to Workforce 2020,* 30.

CHAPTER THREE

Innovations

Technologies with the Potential to Reshape Your Job

Ａll around us, technology works miracles every day. Robotic exoskeletons are helping paraplegics to walk. Surgeons are using virtual reality to perform eye surgery with greater precision than ever before. Robots are going places where it would be dangerous or impossible to humans to venture: into burning buildings and enemy territory during war, and even onto the surface of Mars. Driverless cars are being developed that could bring greater independence to the elderly and disabled, and reduce the number of accidents.

At the same time, technology is reshaping almost every industry and job. It's changing things so fast that workers can no longer expect to remain employable by keeping their heads down and performing the same tasks, year in, year out, no matter how skilled or knowledgeable they are. Right now, no matter where you work or what you do, there's a new technology about to change the way you work forever.

Take accounting, for example. Tax preparation software has reduced the need for accountants, but it's also freed accountants to do more complex and intellectually challenging tasks than filling out simple tax forms. Or think about nurses. Though technology hasn't eliminated nurses' jobs, it's made what they do considerably more complicated. Nurses now have to learn to use such technologies as electronic drug dosing and delivery systems, electronic patient and IV monitors, and electronic health records. And consider the kinds of work you used to do as an intern or a college student or for extra cash in the summertime. Office positions like telephone operator, word processor, and typist have been replaced by automated systems,[1] virtual agent programs are doing call center work,[2] and the Internet and bar coding systems have rendered some library personnel obsolete.[3]

Whatever you do for a living, it's prudent to keep an eye out for technologies that may prove game-changers. To that end, in this chapter we've compiled a list of the top technologies reshaping industries, from ones you use every day, like social media and mobile devices; to those changing the way companies do business, like big data and cloud computing; to those still on the horizon, like space tourism. We've included many examples of inventions with the potential to disrupt sectors, like apps that do the work of bank tellers and travel agents, sensors that exponentially increase the amount of data organizations can collect, and wearable drum kits that just plain make musicians look cooler. And we offer some advice for staying employable in a technology-driven workplace.

Big Data

We inhabit a world teeming with data—data that we have only recently been able to collect. Technologies such as sensors and software can convert such phenomena as Facebook posts, customers' buying habits, patients' blood glucose levels, and the location of packages into useable information. Data-capturing tools have become so advanced, in fact, that we now have access to more information than traditional data processing applications are able to manage, a happening often termed *big data*.[4]

Big data has almost unlimited uses, and it's rapidly changing the way we do business. Retailers, for example, use information streams such as credit card reports, loyalty programs, and visits to websites to track data on customers' demographics and brand preferences. They then use this data to tailor advertisements to specialized groups.[5] If a customer buys prenatal vitamins and maternity clothes at Target, the company starts sending her coupons for diapers and formula.[6] Online grocer Fresh Direct adjusts its prices and promotions daily based on data gleaned from transactions.[7] Ford, Southwest, Pepsi, and other firms continually monitor social media to assess public reaction to their marketing campaigns.[8] In fact, big data can be used for almost anything, including identifying business trends, assessing the quality of research, preventing diseases, linking legal citations, fighting crime, and determining real-time roadway traffic conditions.

When used properly, big data can help companies improve sales figures and increase efficiency. For example, UPS installs sensors on its trucks that track the vehicles' condition, speed, direction, and performance, information that helps the company optimize its delivery routes. In 2010, data from these sensors saved UPS 1.7 million miles of driving and 183,000 gallons of fuel.[9] McKinsey estimates that the US healthcare industry could save over $300 billion each year by using big data to improve efficiency, and that retailers could use it to increase operating margins by over 60%.[10]

Big data will become one of the hot career fields of the future, as millions of workers will be needed to capture, curate, store, search, share, transfer, analyze, and visualize data. By 2015, big data will create a projected 1.9 million IT jobs in the United States and 4.4 million IT jobs worldwide.[11] The McKinsey Global Institute estimates that by 2018, the United States alone could face a shortage of 140,000 to 190,000 people with the deep analytical skills needed to make sense of big data, and lack 1.5 million managers and analysts with the know-how to use big data to make effective decisions.[12]

Soon, even people who aren't mathematicians or statisticians will need to be able to work with big data. Senior executives now describe handling data as an essential competency for leadership. Leaders accustomed to relying on instinct will need to adopt a more scientific mindset, using data to test hypotheses and make predictions.[13] An Institute for the Future report calls this skill *computational thinking*: the ability to understand data-based reasoning and translate large amounts of data into actionable concepts. Computational thinking will be increasingly required of employees at all levels.[14]

Workers will also need to practice what the Institute for the Future terms *cognitive load management,* or coping with the sheer volume of information available to them. Being able to quickly extract meaning from data and interpret it

---

Five Jobs That Could Be Disrupted by Big Data

- *Manufacturing operations manager:* Powerful operations management software can now collect, analyze, and summarize information about all aspects of factory operations, from energy consumption to labor costs to quality issues.[15]

- *Sportswriter:* Companies like Automated Insights of Durham, North Carolina produce software capable of automatically generating customized sports stories. Robbie Allen, founder of Automated Insights, claims his software can cheaply create over 1,000 pieces of content per second.[16]

- *Business analyst:* Applications can now collect and analyze raw corporate data faster than humans can.[17]

- *Executive:* The analysis of data can provide firms with real-time direction and insight, perhaps changing the role of leaders whose job is to give companies direction.[18]

- *Future theorist:* Big data can even help predict such events as political unrest, civil wars, and terrorist strikes—work often performed by futurists.[19]

for various audiences using tools like visualization will become a valued skill.[20] Employees must also be wary of information overload, as multitasking can be detrimental to one's workplace performance: A Stanford study shows that people dealing with several information streams at once do not perform as well as those who concentrate on one thing at a time.[21]

Sensor Technology

From thermometers to electronic water meters, from touch screens to touch lamps, from theft detection tags in stores to smoke detectors in homes, we come into contact with dozens of sensors every day. And sensors are being incorporated into more products all the time. Sensors are attached to car bumpers that set off alarms if a driver's about to back into something. They're imbedded in wearable workout devices that track users' vital signs in real time. Sensors are what convert images to electronic data in digital cameras and what "tell" your tablet whether you're holding it in portrait or landscape mode.

Increasingly, sensors are contributing to the proliferation of big data by transmitting data about almost everything. HP Labs' planned Central Nervous System for the Earth project, as only one example, would attach billions of sensors to buildings, highways, bridges, and many other locations. Data from these sensors could be used to advance knowledge of everything from climate change to oil production to highway infrastructure to seismic events.[22]

Sensor technology is expected to experience massive growth in the near future. In 2010, the market for sensors was worth $8.6 billion, and it's projected to reach $19.5 billion in 2016. Fairchild Semiconductor researcher Janusz Bryzek predicts that sensor technology will contribute to the creation of 6 million jobs, 2 million of them directly involved in designing and building sensors. Bryzek believes sensor technology will be responsible for the next generation of billionaires.[23]

Social Media

Two-thirds of the global Internet population belongs to a social network.[24] More people belong to Facebook than are US citizens.[25] People now spend twice as much time on social networking than any other online activity,[26] and share over 1 billion pieces of content on Facebook each week.[27]

Individuals have embraced social networking, using it to find and share information; connect with family, friends, and community members; and create and distribute media. Companies, too, are using social media for everything from branding to training and development to coordinating project teams. According to think tanks Deloitte and McKinsey, though, organizations have just begun to tap into the potential of social networking.[28] Most companies' social media efforts, they state, are still primarily customer-facing. Companies have realized that online marketing can be just as effective as traditional advertising for a fraction of the cost. Ford, for example, achieved the same brand recognition for its Fiesta model with social media as it would have with a TV campaign—at a tenth of the cost.[29] Firms spent $716 million on social media marketing in 2010, and are expected to increase spending to $3.1 billion by 2014.[30]

Though companies have reaped rich benefits from customer-centered social media initiatives, they may see even more advantages by implementing internal social networks. Such networks allow employees to tap *information flows*, or constantly updated, "living" sources of information like blogs and forums, rather than static *knowledge stocks* like manuals and one-time training courses.[31] They amplify communications, supplementing one-to-one forms of transmission like email and phone calls with many-to-many forms such as wikis.[32] They enable individuals to pose questions and receive timely answers from subject matter experts. And, since social media is archived and searchable, it can give employees access to information once trapped in email inboxes or departmental silos and reduce the amount of time they spend searching for content.[33] According to McKinsey, though 72% of companies use social technologies, the full potential of social media in the workplace is yet unrealized.[34] Properly deployed social media, McKinsey estimates, could increase knowledge workers' productivity by 20% to 25% and recover between $900 billion and $1.3 trillion in value.[35]

Some companies are already using social media internally with great success. Cisco operates the Integrated Workforce Experience, a dashboard where employees can form work communities, find information about projects, track their personal productivity, email and text colleagues, and access wikis, blogs, and forums.[36] Software maker SAP's Developer Network reaches outside the company's walls. Some 1.5 million internal and external stakeholders, including developers, customers, and vendors, participate on this platform. Questions posted to the Developer Network are answered in an average of 17 minutes, and 85% are resolved.[37]

Other companies use social media for training and development. IBM's On Demand Workplace builds real-time learning into the course of the workday in much the same manner as the help function of a software program. Workers can search content tailored to their role, location, and experience level on an as-needed basis, and rate and tag this content to help others assess its value. Some firms allow employees to post informational videos on platforms that resemble internal versions of YouTube.[38]

Social media has also served as an engine of job creation. A study by the University of Maryland found that Facebook alone has created over 235,000 US jobs and added $15.71 billion to the US economy. Some 53,000 people are employed in companies that simply create apps for Facebook.[39] Colleges and universities

> ### Four Jobs That Could Be Disrupted by Social Media
>
> - *TV announcer:* Many popular TV and radio shows are broadcast online rather than through traditional channels, and amateur-driven YouTube is becoming ever more popular as a source for news and information.
>
> - *Gossip columnist:* Celebrities are now spilling their own secrets via Twitter.
>
> - *Newspaper writer:* Much of today's reporting is shared in real time through blogs and news feeds.
>
> - *Publicist:* Websites such as the *Huffington Post* reach larger populations than many traditional newspapers, and writers who post diligently can become instant icons. People who score regular video spots on the *Huffington Post* or are LinkedIn thought leaders become famous without publicists.

have responded to the rise of social media by launching programs and majors in the subject, with schools of journalism offering concentrations in online public relations, social media, and social media management and specialties in social networks and web development for social media.[40]

Mobile Computing

The desktop computer may be going the way of the landline. At home and at work, more and more people are adopting mobile technologies. Over 6 billion people worldwide own mobile phones[41]—more than have access to clean toilets[42]—and the number of cell phones will exceed the Earth's population by 2014.[43] By 2015, a projected 788 million people will exclusively use mobile technology to access the Internet.[44] More than just trendy gadgets, mobile devices have become part of the fabric of everyday lives: 73% of male and 63% of female smartphone owners say they can't go an hour without checking their phones.[45]

An essential component of mobile computing is the application, or app, a piece of software designed to run on mobile devices like tablets or smartphones. Apps exist for everything from gaming to weather to traffic to photo sharing to healthcare information. They're extraordinarily popular: Some 775,000 of them have been created for the iPhone alone, and to date, they've been downloaded from Apple's App Store 40 billion times.[46]

Apps are also a moneymaking opportunity. Apple has paid out $7 billion to app developers since its App Store launched in 2008.[47] Though consumers pay for some apps, they increasingly expect to download them for free. Developers can still make money off them, however, by offering them as part of a subscription or collecting advertising revenues.[48] One study found that 73% of Android apps are free, and that 80% rely on advertising.[49] Firms in a wide variety of industries, in-

---

Five Jobs That Could Be Disrupted by Mobile Technology

- *Weather forecaster:* Weather apps provide users with current and forecasted weather information, alerts, updates, maps, and travel weather details.

- *Wedding photographer:* Wedding photography apps allow users to edit, enhance, and share photographs.[50]

- *Concierge:* Hotel apps let guests manage all aspects of their stay, including booking, ordering room service, requesting housekeeping and valet parking, and reserving spa treatments and room amenities.[51] Apps have been developed for use in malls that do the work of customer service agents, providing shoppers with directions and answers to their questions.[52]

- *Bank teller:* More banks are offering apps which let customers pay bills, transfer funds, view and balance accounts, deactivate lost or stolen banking cards, find ATMs, and make better financial decisions.[53]

- *Security guard:* New apps have been developed that allow employees to sign in using photographs, voice recognition, or unique security codes.[54]

---

cluding healthcare, consulting, law, staffing, and finance, are also looking to hire app developers, app developer project managers, and app consultants.

Cloud Computing

The term *cloud computing* refers to software and other services hosted remotely on a network which consumers can "rent" rather than buy and install on their own devices. Well-known examples of cloud services include Dropbox, a file-sharing application, and Google Play, a system which allows users to store their music, apps, books, and movies in a digital "cloud" rather than on their computers. Companies and individual users are drawn to cloud computing because it lets them access files and media on multiple devices, and store them independently of hardware which may crash or be damaged. Cloud computing also makes it cheaper and less labor-intensive for businesses to acquire new applications. Rather than investing heavily in servers, software, and IT, they can simply buy software from outside vendors who will maintain it for them.[55] It's been estimated that, by 2020, more people will use cloud-based software than software they've installed onto their devices.[56]

Cloud computing is big business. The market for cloud computing services grew from $3.4 billion in 2011 to $5 billion in 2012, and, according to Gartner's 2011 CEO Agenda Survey, by 2020 the majority of organizations will rely on the cloud for more than half of their IT services.[57] New jobs are being created to manage and maintain cloud systems, such as cloud architects, cloud capacity planners, cloud services managers, and cloud business solutions consultants.[58] A review

---

Five Jobs That Could Be Disrupted by Cloud Computing

Cloud computing may mean that companies have less need for some internal IT positions, including:

- On-site help desk technicians
- Telecommunications technicians
- Systems administrators
- IT trainers
- Technical training managers

At the same time, cloud providers may be hiring more people with IT skills to service their clients.

---

of DICE and Indeed job boards shows that cloud-related positions are already in demand: Desirable employers like Amazon, Hewlett-Packard, Facebook, and Salesforce.com are looking for cloud engineers, systems administrators, software development engineers, as well as cloud helpdesk personnel, contract managers, and database administrators.

And cloud computing is revolutionizing IT. Delegating routine upkeep tasks to cloud providers frees companies' IT departments to focus on innovation, analytics, and decision making. To cope with the rise of cloud software, IT professionals will need to develop different competencies, such as managing a network of cloud providers, redesigning their firms' infrastructure to accommodate cloud services, and supporting employee learning on cloud platforms. In short, the cloud means that IT professionals will focus less on supporting systems and more on supporting services.[59]

Smart Machines

Thanks to smart machines like robots, voice-activated technology, and computers like IBM's Watson that can beat humans at *Jeopardy!*, our present is looking more and more like yesterday's science fiction. Long a mainstay of the manufacturing industry, robotics is moving into other arenas, such as healthcare. The *da Vinci*® robotic platform assists doctors in performing surgery, while Japan's "nursebot" Twendy-One can carry people, clean floors, and bring patients meals on a tray.[60] Google's driverless car has accelerated industry timelines for the production of autonomous vehicles.[61] Rethink Robotics' Baxter robot, designed to carry out a variety of repetitive tasks, can adapt to its environment, learn new tasks in under 30 minutes, and work safely alongside humans. Its low price point may make it a viable alternative to offshoring for American manufacturers.[62]

Though many of these smart machines are still in early stages of development, they've sparked fears that they will take jobs from humans. After all, in

> ### Five Jobs That Could Be Disrupted by Robots and Other Smart Machines
>
> - *Housekeeper:* Robotic vacuums, window cleaners, lawnmowers, pool cleaners, pet feeders, and dusters can perform many simple household tasks.[63]
>
> - *Taxi driver:* The day of the driverless car is not far off. Its precursors are already here: Airplanes use autopilot and airlines have automated people movers that transfer travelers between terminals. Google is pursuing taxi permits for its driverless car in San Francisco and Las Vegas, and limos, trucks, and trains may be the next vehicles to be automated. Such vehicles could reduce the number of accidents, as a mechanized "driver" could never be distracted by an incoming text or an obnoxious ad on the radio, and they could help the elderly and disabled become more independent.[64]
>
> - *Manufacturing line worker:* Manufacturing has come a long way from the days when *I Love Lucy's* Lucy and Ethel scrambled to keep up with chocolates moving along a conveyor belt. Today, robots perform many functions once carried out by factory workers, including welding, painting, assembly, packing, palletizing, and picking and placing. Many factories are almost completely automated.[65]
>
> - *Rescue worker:* The US military uses a robot called the BEAR to move injured soldiers away from areas under attack and to enter buildings that may contain toxins or explosive materials.[66] It's also testing a walking robot called BigDog which can carry 400 pounds for 24 hours without refueling, acts as a mobile charging station for batteries, and may someday respond to simple verbal commands like a dog.[67]
>
> - *Surgeon:* Smart machines have long been used in healthcare for surgery, rehabilitation, telepresence, and dosing and delivering medications.[68]

recent years, certain jobs have been lost to automation and digitization. ATMs have reduced the need for bank tellers, for example, and self-checkout machines for cashiers. Many of the jobs predicted to be in greatest decline through 2020 fall into this category: semiconductor processors; textile knitting and weaving machine, switchboard, and sewing machine operators; and postal workers (electronic communications and automated bill payments have reduced the volume of mail), to name a few.[69] Some futurists even predict that robots could put humans out of work by 2045.[70]

But smart machines are also creating jobs in such sectors as manufacturing, business, and healthcare. A study by the International Federation of Robotics estimates that 900,000 to 1.5 million jobs will be created in the robotics field between 2012 and 2016, and 1 to 2 million more between 2017 and 2020.[71] While most of these jobs will require engineering and software backgrounds, many people will also be needed to manufacture, sell, market, and oversee the distribution of smart machines.[72]

Smart machines also have the potential to free humans do to the kinds of work they are uniquely good at: work that involves creativity, innovation, and personal interaction. As smart machines become more prevalent, demand for skills that can't be automated will rise. In particular, employers will seek workers skilled at what the Institute for the Future terms *sense-making*, or being able to scan your environment for data, determine which information is useful and which is not, and make decisions accordingly. Sense-makers are able to determine the deeper meaning or significance behind raw data.

Virtual and Augmented Reality

Once the stuff of science fiction—think of *Star Trek*'s holodeck—virtual reality is getting more sophisticated all the time. Defined as a computer-created artificial environment in which outcomes are partly determined by a user's actions,[73] virtual reality is now used for everything from entertainment to surgery. Games like World of Warcraft and the forthcoming EVE: Valkyrie place the player in a fully-realized alternate world, while Nintendo's Wii U allows players to manipulate actions on the screen using gestures or wireless controllers. The US military, the aviation industry, and some medical schools use virtual reality to train soldiers, pilots, and doctors. Virtual reality has even been used to help people overcome phobias by placing them in realistic simulations that mimic the situations they fear.

A close cousin to virtual reality, *augmented reality* refers to the enhancement of the real world through the use of computer-generated data, sounds, graphics, videos, and other media. This data and media may be displayed on a monitor or handheld device or even overlaid across a user's field of vision by a head-mounted device, pair of eyeglasses, or contact lenses.[74] Google Glass, for instance, projects information such as maps, directions, the time, and answers to Internet searches in front of what its user is seeing in the real world.[75]

Juniper Research predicts that augmented reality applications will generate close to $300 million in global revenues by 2013.[76]

Solar Energy

Interested in a job that helps the planet? Then a career in solar energy may be for you. The solar sector is taking off, with installations of solar panels more than doubling year after year. The United States now has the capacity to power more than 1.3 million homes with solar energy, and more people will be needed to design, install, sell, and service solar panels.[77] According to the Solar Foundation, 119,000 people are employed in the US solar industry, and, over the next year, 45% of solar firms are expected to add jobs for a total of over 20,000 new solar workers.[78]

> ### Five Jobs That Could Be Disrupted by Virtual and Augmented Reality
>
> - *Flight instructor:* Virtual reality is widely used in training simulations, including those for flying aircraft.
>
> - *Real estate agent:* Layar, a geolocation-based app, uses GPS, compasses, and other sensors in users' mobile phones to automatically provide them with information on their current location, such as local Tweets and Flickr photos. Home buyers may soon be using it to scope out potential new neighborhoods.[79]
>
> - *Tour guide:* Stella Artois Le Bar Guide is one of many augmented reality applications that help tourists find sites in real time—in this case, bars and restaurants serving Stella Artois beer.[80]
>
> - *Retail clerk:* Ray-Ban's virtual mirror lets shoppers virtually try on sunglasses using their web cameras. The application measures points on customers' faces to size the glasses and help shoppers select a style in half the time it would take at a local retailer.[81]
>
> - *Car salesperson:* BMW's new mobile advertising campaign lets customers virtually drive its electric cars through New York, San Francisco, London, Boston, or Los Angeles.[82]

Job prospects are best for those living in California, the leading state in solar energy and home to over 43,700 solar jobs and some 547,000 houses powered by the sun.[83] Two California cities, Sebastopol and Lancaster, even require that all new buildings and building additions incorporate solar voltaic panels.[84]

Solar industry workers specialize in such areas as research, development, sales, materials manufacturing, construction, operation, and installation and maintenance. Solar engineers, materials scientists, and project developers make excellent salaries. People interested in careers in the solar field who lack STEM backgrounds can start by earning certificates in solar sales or installation from the National Association of Certified Energy Practitioners.[85]

Wearable Technology

From fanciful to functional, wearable technology is becoming a hot commodity. A variant of mobile technology, wearable technology incorporates sensors and other devices into clothing, accessories, and gadgets that users wear right on their bodies. Some forms of wearable technology are purely entertaining, like T-shirts that play the drums or bikinis that use solar power to charge cell phones. Others

Five Jobs That Could Be Disrupted by Wearable Technology

- *Golf caddy:* Game Golf is a wearable device which uses accelerometers, gyroscopes, GPS, and near field communications to monitor golf games, tracking the location of shots, the distance the ball travels, and which clubs a player uses.[86] The SensoGlove uses built-in sensors to gauge the pressure of players' grips, helping them improve their swings.[87]

- *Musician:* The Beat Glove lets wearers tap out music using their fingers, which they hear on a computer.[88] The Electronic Drum Machine T-Shirt features a real working drum machine and looper, and can record loops of up to 3 minutes in length. (And, yes, you can remove the electronics when the shirt goes in the wash.)[89]

- *Personal trainer:* Jawbone's UP wristband automatically tracks wearers' sleeping, eating, and exercise habits, then displays their data on a mobile app. Wearers can use that data to work towards health and fitness goals.[90]

- *Physician:* Preventice's BodyGuardian Remote Monitoring System contains small wearable sensors that transmit key biometric data, such as heart and respiration rates, to patients' doctors. AiQ Smart Clothing has sensors woven right into its fabric.[91]

- *Fashion designer:* Dresses and purses have been developed that use solar power to recharge wearers' electronics.[92] CuteCircuit's Twitter dress displays tweets in real time while being worn.[93]

are more practical, such as wearable sensors that help diabetics keep track of their glucose levels throughout the day.

But, in whatever form it takes, wearable technology is a growing trend. Some 14 million wearable devices were shipped in 2010,[94] and it's been estimated that 100 million wearable medical devices and 80 million wearable sports and fitness devices will be in circulation by 2016.[95] Research firm Gartner predicts that wearable technology will be a $10 billion industry by 2016.[96]

Underwater Technology

Oceans cover 71% of the planet, but only recently have we been able to tap the vast potential of this realm. New technologies like robots and submersibles have made it possible to build structures both above and below the ocean's surface, a boon to nations looking to expand their oil and gas reserves. Oceangoing technologies have also opened up the seas to exploration by scientists and filmmakers. As these technologies advance, more careers will be created for people who love travel or simply being in or on the water, especially those with a scientific bent.

Some up-and-coming underwater careers include:

- *Underwater welding.* Shipbuilding, oil, and gas companies worldwide need divers who are capable of welding underwater. These jobs, while very dangerous, are extremely lucrative, paying anywhere from $15,000 to $150,000 a month. They require both a diving and a welding certificate, and candidates can train at specialized schools such as Divers Academy.[97]

- *Underwater robotics.* Undersea mining is driving the development of sophisticated underwater robots. The underwater robotics market is expected to grow 7% by 2016.[98]

- *Jobs in the autonomous underwater vehicle (AUV) industry.* AUVs—robots which can travel independently underwater—are used by oil and gas companies to inspect pipelines and map the ocean floor, and by the military for surveillance, reconnaissance, mine countermeasures, and anti-submarine warfare. AUV manufacturing is a booming industry, one which saw 13.8% revenue growth between 2008 and 2013.[99]

- *Marine contracting.* Like land-based contractors, marine contractors supervise construction and demolition projects that take place over or under water, such as bridges, tunnels, docks, marinas, and offshore drilling platforms. Marine contracting is a growing industry in need of new entrants with solid STEM backgrounds.[100] Civil, structural, and military engineers, in particular, may find it a great opportunity for a career change.[101]

- *Underwater archeology.* Underwater archeologists study such sites as shipwrecks and sunken cities. Over 15 universities now offer programs in underwater archaeology or related fields such as maritime studies or naval history.[102]

- *Underwater photographers and filmographers.* Jobs for photographers, including those who work underwater, are expected to increase 13% by 2020. Television production companies, marine life magazines, and corporations involved in underwater salvaging are all looking for underwater photographers. The field requires diving certifications, and pay is determined by experience and how deep divers are able to go, but usually ranges from $35,000 to $60,000 a year.[103]

- *Jobs in the hospitality field.* Underwater tour guides lead swims with sea life, while divers teach classes, lead expeditions, and clean tanks in aquariums and theme parks. Restaurants and hotels have even been built underwater that let tourists dine or relax under the sea. Visitors to the Florida Keys, for example, can dive 21 feet below the surface to stay at the

Jules Undersea Lodge,[104] while plush underwater resorts are being built in Dubai, Fiji, and the Maldives.[105]

Space Tourism

Space tourism might sound like something that will only be possible in the distant future, but actually, its day is close at hand. Since the first space tourist launched in 2001, private companies have made significant strides towards making space tourism possible on a larger scale. Virgin Galactic, which launched its first passenger-carrying spaceship, the *VSS Enterprise*, in 2009,[106] has collected about $60 million in deposits for suborbital flights that will give tourists a few minutes of weightlessness and a spectacular view of Earth against the black backdrop of space. Space Adventures Ltd. has taken five people on trips to the International Space Station,[107] while billionaire Robert Bigelow is building a space hotel and Virgin Galactic is constructing a spaceport in New Mexico.[108]

Though, right now, space tourism is only for the super-rich—those jaunts to the International Space Station cost $20 million—space travel is beginning to open up to other customers, such as universities and research organizations that want to perform experiments high above Earth.[109] Like most technologies, space travel should become cheaper and accessible to more people as it matures. The FAA predicts that space tourism will become a $1 billion industry by 2022.[110] Researchers at Spacefuture.com are more optimistic. They're projecting that by 2030 5 million passengers a year will tour space and 70,000 people will live in Earth's orbit. Space tourism could create jobs in such areas as manufacturing, vehicle operations and maintenance, construction, hospitality, insurance, and other industries.[111]

Employability in a Technology-Based World

Technology can be daunting, especially for those of us who didn't grow up with computers and the Internet. One thing to remember is that your subject matter expertise is still needed, as are many of the skills you cultivated offline, such as critical thinking and problem solving. The key is to find ways to use those skills and that expertise *with* technology—what some MIT authors refer to as competing with machines, rather than competing against machines.

Here are some tips for staying afloat in a technology-based economy:

- *Keep on top of industry trends.* All industries today are now shaped by technology to one degree or another. For example, manufacturing has been impacted by 3-D printing, media by video and social networking, and medicine by robotics and virtual reality. These new technologies are the key to employability. By staying informed about them, you'll be better able to anticipate where tomorrow's job opportunities will be. You can keep current with the trends in your industry by reading blog posts and research-based articles published by key associations.

- *Learn about—or even learn how to use—the top technologies in your industry.* Understanding the technologies that are reshaping your field will increase your employment options and put you in a better position to advance both your sector and your career. For instance, though 3-D printing is expected to eliminate many manufacturing jobs, it will also create jobs for those in the manufacturing sector who know how to use it.

- *Take advantage of any training your employer offers, especially when it involves technology.* Ask about classes, programs, or on-the-job training opportunities. Many firms offer free training as part of professional development programs.

- *Pursue free and low-cost training on your own.* Technology retailers often hold free public seminars on their technologies. Microsoft offers personalized training on its products for $100 a year which includes three books and 52 hours of one-on-one counseling.

- *Learn online.* Online tutorials are another excellent way to increase your knowledge and skills. Almost all software and apps today include video tutorials, and YouTube has become an incredible repository of video tutorials from technology providers, consultants, and independent experts. Lynda.com offers over 2,000 video courses on technology, business, and arts topics for as little as $25 a month. Subscribers can watch video tutorials aimed at a variety of user levels, from beginner to expert, on subjects like 3-D animation, photography, graphic design, social media, and software like Excel, Acrobat, Illustrator, and Photoshop.

- *Make lateral moves.* If you've been in one role for a long time, it may be a good idea to try working in another part of your firm. Many companies now value well-rounded employees with expertise in different departments. Lateral moves can enhance your skills, increase your visibility, and provide you with networking opportunities.

- *Network.* Get to know people who are learning or already have the skills and knowledge you're interested in. One way to do so is through Meetup, a website which helps groups of people with shared interests form clubs and plan meetings. There are groups available centered around everything from hiking to business growth to technology to wine and food. Meetup is free to join, as are many of the events hosted by its groups.

Notes

1. Associated Press, "Can Smart Machines Take Your Job? Middle Class Jobs Increasingly Being Replaced By Technology," *New York Daily News*, January 24, 2013, http://www.nydailynews.com/news/national/smart-machines-job-article-1.1246522.

2. Mark Gaydos, "Virtual Agents Will Replace Live Customer Services Reps. Pro: Clearly Destined," *Businessweek*, accessed August 1, 2013, http://www.businessweek.com/debateroom/archives/2010/07/virtual_agents_will_replace_live_customer_service_reps.html.

3. College Online, "Are Librarians Totally Obsolete?" *College Online*, accessed August 3, 2013, http://www.collegeonline.org/library/adult-continued-education/librarians-needed.html.

4. Institute for the Future and Apollo Research Institute, *Future of Work Report: Data-Intensive Work* (Palo Alto, CA: Institute for the Future; Phoenix, AZ: Apollo Research Institute, 2012), 1–2, http://apolloresearchinstitute.com/sites/default/files/future-of-work-report-data-intensive_work.pdf (site discontinued); James Manyika et al., *Big Data: The Next Frontier for Innovation, Competition, and Productivity* (Washington, DC: McKinsey Global Institute, 2011), 5; Marcia Conner, "Time to Build Your Big-Data Muscles," *Fast Company*, July 17, 2012, http://www.fastcompany.com/1842928/time-build-your-big-data-muscles.

5. Institute for the Future and Apollo Research Institute, *Data-Intensive Work,* 1–2; Conner, "Time to Build Your Big-Data Muscles."

6. Charles Duhigg, "How Companies Learn Your Secrets," *New York Times*, February 16, 2012, http://www.nytimes.com/2012/02/19/magazine/shopping-habits.html?pagewanted=all&_r=0.

7. Jacques Bugin, Michael Chui, and James Manyika, "Clouds, Big Data, and Smart Assets: Ten Tech-Enabled Business Trends to Watch," *McKinsey Quarterly*, August 2010, https://www.mckinseyquarterly.com/Clouds_big_data_and_smart_assets_Ten_tech-enabled_business_trends_to_watch_2647.

8. Ibid.

9. "Telematics," UPS.com, accessed December 20, 2012, http://www.ups.com/content/us/en/bussol/browse/leadership-telematics.html.

10. Bugin, Chui, and Manyika, "Clouds, Big Data, and Smart Assets."

11. Patrick Thibodeau, "Big Data to Create 1.9M IT Jobs in U.S. by 2015, Says Gartner," *Computerworld*, October 22, 2012, http://www.computerworld.com/s/article/9232721/Big_data_to_create_1.9M_IT_jobs_in_U.S._by_2015_says_Gartner.

12. James Manyika et al., *Big Data*, 5.

13. Conner, "Time to Build Your Big-Data Muscles."

14. Institute for the Future for Apollo Research Institute, *Future Work Skills 2020* (Palo Alto, CA: Institute for the Future, 2011), 4, 10, http://www.iftf.org/uploads/media/SR-1382A_UPRI_future_work_skills_sm.pdf.

15. Associated Press, "More Data and the Cloud Help Replace Humans—And Their Salaries—On The Job," *Omaha World Herald*, January 24, 2013, http://www.omaha.com/article/20130124/MONEY/701249997/1707.

16. Ibid.

17. Michael Vizard, "Big Data and the Demise of Business Analysts," *Slashdot*, February 4, 2013, http://slashdot.org/topic/bi/big-data-and-the-demise-of-business-analysts/.

18. Mick Yates, "Big Data Kills the Pilot?" *LeaderValues* (blog), May 26, 2013, http://www.leader-values.com/wordpress/?p=6270.

19. Ibid., 12.

20. Cisco, *Transitioning to Workforce 2020* (San Jose, CA: Cisco, 2011), 11, http://www.cisco.com/web/learning/employer_resources/pdfs/Workforce_2020_White_Paper.pdf.

21. Ian Steadman, "Big Data and the Death of the Theorist," *Wired*, January 25, 2013, http://www.wired.co.uk/news/archive/2013-01/25/big-data-end-of-theory.

22. Greg Lindsay, "HP Invests a 'Central Nervous System for Earth' and Joins the Smarter Planet Sweepstakes," *FastCompany*, accessed August 3, 2013, http://www.fastcompany.com/1548674/hp-invents-central-nervous-system-earth-and-joins-smarter-planet-sweepstakes.

23. Janusz Bryzek, "Emergences of a $Trillion MEMS Sensor Market," Fairchild Semiconductor (presentation slides), http://www.sensorscon.org/English/Archives/201203/Presentations/Janusz_Bryzek_SensorsCon2012.pdf.

24. Jeanne C. Meister and Karie Willyerd, *The 2020 Workplace: How Innovative Companies Attract, Develop, and Keep Tomorrow's Employees Today* (New York: HarperBusiness, 2010), Kindle edition, chap. 4.

25. Ibid.

26. Institute for the Future for Apollo Research Institute, *Future Work Skills 2020* (Palo Alto, CA: Institute for the Future; Phoenix, AZ: Apollo Research Institute, 2011), 8, http://www.iftf.org/uploads/media/SR-1382A_UPRI_future_work_skills_sm.pdf.

27. Meister and Willyerd, *2020 Workplace*, chap. 4.

28. McKinsey Global Institute, *The Social Economy: Unlocking Value and Productivity Through Social Technology. Executive Summary* (Washington, DC: McKinsey Global Institute, 2012), 3, http://www.mckinsey.com/insights/mgi/research/technology_and_innovation/the_social_economy; Deloitte, *The 2011 Shift Index* (New York: Deloitte, 2011), 4, http://www.deloitte.com/assets/Dcom-UnitedStates/Local%20Assets/Documents/TMT_us_tmt/us_tmt_shiftindex_revised_120512.pdf.

29. Adrian Ott, "How Social Media Has Changed the Workplace," *Fast Company*, November 11, 2012, http://www.fastcompany.com/1701850/how-social-media-has-changed-workplace-study.

30. Deloitte, *2011 Shift Index*, 103-4.

31. Ibid., 23.

32. McKinsey Global Institute, *Social Economy*, 11.

33. Deloitte, *2011 Shift Index*, 8; Holmes, "Can't-Miss Social Media Trends."

34. McKinsey Global Institute, *Social Economy*, 3.

35. Ibid.

36. Cisco, *Transitioning to Workforce 2020*, 12.

37. Deloitte, *2011 Shift Index*, 23.

38. Meister and Willyerd, *2020 Workplace*, chap. 7.

39. Il-Horn Hann, Siva Viswanathan, and Byungwan Koh, *The Facebook App Economy* (College Park, MD: Robert H. Smith School of Business at the University of Maryland, 2011), 6, http://www.rhsmith.umd.edu/news/releases/2011/091911.aspx.

40. "Social Media Careers," Journalism Degree.com, accessed August 3, 2013, http://www.journalismdegree.com/social-media-careers/.

41. Joshua Pramis, "Number of Mobile Phones to Exceed World Population," *Digital Trends*, February 28, 2013, http://www.digitaltrends.com/mobile/mobile-phone-world-population-2014/.

42. Iowa Future, "Iowa, Did You Know?" *YouTube* video, 7:38, uploaded August 4, 2011, http://www.youtube.com/watch?v=dMsNct4X_GU.

43. Pramis, "Phones to Exceed World Population."

44. Ethan Hale, "Your Company Needs a Mobile Strategy Yesterday—And These Numbers Prove It," *Fast Company*, October 3, 2012, http://www.fastcompany.com/3001816/your-company-needs-mobile-strategy-yesterday-and-these-numbers-prove-it.

45. Trendwatching, "December 2012 Trend Briefing: 10 Crucial Consumer Trends for 2013," accessed December 8, 2012, http://www.trendwatching.com/trends/10trends2013/.

46. TJ McCue, "10 Leading Finance and Banking Apps for iPhone and iPad," *Forbes*, January 8, 2013, http://www.forbes.com/sites/tjmccue/2013/01/08/10-leading-finance-and-banking-apps-for-iphone-and-ipad/.

47. Ibid.

48. John Manoogian III, "How Free Apps Can Make More Money Than Paid Apps," *TechCrunch*, August 26, 2012, http://techcrunch.com/2012/08/26/how-free-apps-can-make-more-money-than-paid-apps/.

49. Ingrid Lunden, "In Mobile Apps, Free Ain't Free, But Cambridge University Has a Plan to Fix It," *TechCrunch*, March 6, 2012, http://techcrunch.com/2012/03/06/in-mobile-apps-free-aint-free-but-cambridge-university-has-a-plan-to-fix-it/.

50. Joanne Carter, "Top 10 iPad and iPhone Wedding Photography Apps," *The App Whisperer*, May 29, 2011, http://theappwhisperer.com/2011/05/29/top-10-ipad-and-iphone-wedding-photography-apps/.

51. Jimmy Im, "Will Conrad's New Concierge App Replace the Real Thing?" *HotelChatter*, December 18, 2012, http://www.hotelchatter.com/story/2012/12/17/163345/56/hotels/Will_Conrad's_New_Concierge_App_Replace_The_Real_Thing%3F.

52. Anton Troianovski, "Apps: The New Corporate Cost-Cutting Tool," *Wall Street Journal*, March 5, 2013, http://online.wsj.com/article/SB10001424127887324678604578342690460880894.html.

53. Penny Crosman and Mary Wisniewski, "Top 10 Mobile Banking Apps," *American Banker*, February 25, 2013, http://www.americanbanker.com/gallery/top-ten-mobile-banking-apps-1057018-1.html.

54. "MicroStrategy Makes Mobile App to Replace Employee Photo Badge," *Washington Business Journal*, accessed August 3, 2013, http://www.bizjournals.com/washington/blog/techflash/2013/04/microstrategy-makes-mobile-app-to.html.

55. Bugin, Chui, and Manyika, "Clouds, Big Data, and Smart Assets."

56. Tracey Wilen-Daugenti, *Society 3.0: How Technology Is Reshaping Education, Work and Society* (New York: Peter Lang, 2012), 129.

57. Nick Heath, "Cloud Computing: What Does It Really Mean for IT Jobs?," *TechRepublic*, August 8, 2012, http://www.techrepublic.com/blog/cio-insights/cloud-computing-what-does-it-really-mean-for-it-jobs/39749168.

58. Joe McKendrick, "How Cloud Computing Is Changing Many Job Descriptions," *Forbes*, December 26, 2011, http://www.forbes.com/sites/joemckendrick/2011/12/26/cloud-computing-is-changing-many-job-descriptions/.

59. "How Cloud Computing Is Changing the IT Industry," *Seattle Post-Intelligencer*, June 13, 2013, http://www.seattlepi.com/business/article/How-Cloud-Computing-is-Changing-the-IT-Industry-4263418.php.

60. Corey Binns, "Twendy-One Nursebot Says Sit Up and Eat Your Jell-O," *Popsci*, July 8, 2009, http://www.popsci.com/scitech/article/2009-06/machines-heal.

61. Institute for the Future for Apollo Research Institute, *Future of Work Report: Smart Machines* (Palo Alto, CA: Institute for the Future; Phoenix, AZ: Apollo Research Institute, 2012), 1-2, http://apolloresearchinstitute.com/research-studies/workforce-preparedness/future-work-skills-2020-cognitive-load-management (site discontinued).

62. Anita Li, "Meet Baxter: A Robot With Common Sense," *Mashable*, September 19, 2012, http://mashable.com/2012/09/19/baxter-robot-work/.

63. "Personal and Domestic Robots," RobotShop, accessed August 3, 2013, http://www.robotshop.com/personal-domestic-robots.html.

64. "The Autonomous Vehicle Technology," *DL-ERC*, accessed August 3, 2013, http://www.dl-erc. org/component/content/article/1-electronic-research-collection-category/4-the-autonomous-vehicle-technology.

65. Aaron Saenz, "No Humans, Just Robots—Amazing Videos of the Modern Factory," *Singularity Hub,* February 11, 2010, http://singularityhub.com/2010/02/11/no-humans-just-robots-amazing-videos-of-the-modern-factory/.

66. Mark Rutherford, "BEAR Robot Roars to the Rescue," *CNET*, August 22, 2009, http://news. cnet.com/8301-13639_3-10315369-42.html.

67. "Robotic 'Mule,' DARPA's LS3 Model, May Aid Soldiers," InnovationNewsDaily Staff, *Huffington Post*, February 8, 2012, http://www.huffingtonpost.com/2012/02/08/ls3-robot-mule_n_1263726.html.

68. *Wikipedia*, s.v. "Medical Robots," last modified March 19, 2013, http://en.wikipedia.org/wiki/ Medical_robots.

69. Boston.com and Monster.com, "10 Jobs in Decline through 2020," accessed December 5, 2012, http://www.boston.com/jobs/galleries/10_jobs_in_decline/.

70. Jason Dorrier, "Moshe Vardi: Robots Could Put Humans Out of Work By 2045," *Singularity Hub*, May 15, 2013, http://singularityhub.com/2013/05/15/moshe-vardi-robots-could-put-humans-out-of-work-by-2045/.

71. Peter Gorle and Andrew Clive, *Positive Impact of Industrial Robots on Employment* (Frankfurt, Germany: International Federation of Robotics), 3, http://www.ifr.org/uploads/media/ Update_Study_Robot_creates_Jobs_2013.pdf.

72. "Robotics Industry Fueling Job Growth," RobotWorx, accessed August 3, 2013, http://www. robots.com/blog/viewing/robotics-industry-fueling-job-growth.

73. *Merriam-Webster*, s.v. "Virtual Reality," accessed August 3, 2013, http://www.merriam-webster. com/dictionary/virtual%20reality.

74. *Wikipedia*, s.v. "Augmented Reality," last modified July 30, 2013, http://en.wikipedia.org/ wiki/Augmented_reality.

75. "Glass. What It Does," Google, accessed August 3, 2013, http://www.google.com/glass/start/ what-it-does/.

76. Juniper Research, "Augmented Reality Mobile Apps to Generate Nearly $300mn in Revenues, Juniper Report Finds," news release, November 6, 2012, https://www.juniperresearch.com/ press-releases.php/http:/press-releases.php?category=2.

77. Solar Energy Industries Association, *Solar Energy Facts: Q1 2013* (Washington, DC: Solar Energy Industries Association, 2013), 1, http://www.seia.org/sites/default/files/Q1%202013%20 SMI%20Fact%20Sheetv3.pdf.

78. The Solar Foundation, *National Solar Jobs Census 2012* (Washington, DC: The Solar Foundation, 2012), 5, http://thesolarfoundation.org/sites/thesolarfoundation.org/files/TSF%20 Solar%20Jobs%20Census%202012%20Final.pdf.

79. Jesus Diaz, "Layar: First Mobile Augmented Reality Browser Is Your Real Life HUD," *Gizmodo*, June 16, 2009, http://gizmodo.com/5292748/layar-first-mobile-augmented-reality-browser-is-your-real-life-hud; John Herrman, "Android's Best Augmented Reality App Hits the iPhone," *Gizmodo*, October 14, 2009, http://gizmodo.com/5381846/androids-best-augmented-reality-app-hits-the-iphone.

80. Stella Artois, "Stella Artois Launches Le Bar Guide," news release, accessed August 3, 2013, http://www.ab-inbev.com/pdf/SA_BarGuide.pdf.

81. Cory O'Brien, "Ray-Ban Uses Augmented Reality for Their Virtual Mirror," *The Future of Ads* (blog), accessed August 3, 2013, http://thefutureofads.com/ray-ban-uses-augmented-reality-for-their-virtual-mirror.

82. Kurt Ernst, "BMW Works to Perfect the Virtual Test Drive," *MotorAuthority*, April 24, 2012, http://www.motorauthority.com/news/1075654_bmw-works-to-perfect-the-virtual-test-drive.

83. The Solar Foundation, "State Solar Jobs," infographic, accessed August 3, 2012, http://thesolarfoundation.org/solarstates#ca.

84. Miranda Green, "California Towns Pass Law Requiring New Buildings to Have Solar Panels," *Daily Beast*, May 10, 2013, http://www.thedailybeast.com/articles/2013/05/10/california-towns-pass-law-requiring-new-buildings-to-have-solar-panels.html.

85. "Get Certified," North American Board of Certified Energy Practitioners, accessed August 3, 2013, http://www.nabcep.org/certification.

86. Home page, SensoGlove, accessed August 3, 2013, http://www.sensoglove.com/.

87. "BeatGlove," Jacek Spiewla.com, accessed August 3, 2013, http://www.jacekspiewla.com/projects/beatglove/.

88. "Electronic Drum Machine Shirt," ThinkGeek, accessed August 3, 2013, http://www.thinkgeek.com/product/ebb1/#tabs.

89. "UP," Jawbone, accessed August 3, 2013, https://jawbone.com/up.

90. Michelle McNickle, "10 Wearable Health Tech Devices to Watch," *Information Week*, October 31, 2012, http://www.informationweek.com/healthcare/mobile-wireless/10-wearable-health-tech-devices-to-watch/240012613.

91. Jasmin Malik Chua, "LED-Equipped Solar Timbuk2 Bag Creates a FLAP at PopTech," *Ecouterre*, October 23, 2009, http://www.ecouterre.com/led-equipped-solar-timbuk2-bag-creates-a-flap-at-poptech/.

92. Ellie Krupnick, "Twitter Dress: Nicole Scherzinger Debuts Electronic Outfit by CuteCircuit," *Huffington Post*, November 2, 2012, http://www.huffingtonpost.com/2012/11/02/twitter-dress-nicole-scherzinger-photos_n_2064299.html.

93. Johanna Mischke, "Wearable Technology Creates Significant Growth Opportunities," *Wearable Technologies,* August 5, 2012, http://www.wearable-technologies.com/2012/08/wearable-technology-creates-significant-growth-opportunities/.

94. McNickle, "Wearable Health Tech Devices."

95. Kelli B. Grant, "Watch Out for Wearable Tech," *MarketWatch*, April 17, 2013, http://www.marketwatch.com/story/watch-out-for-wearable-tech-2013-04-17.

96. Home page, Game Golf, accessed August 3, 2013, http://www.gameyourgame.com/.

97. "The Global Job Market for Underwater Welders," Underwater Welding Guide, March 30, 2012, http://underwaterweldingguide.wordpress.com/2012/03/30/the-global-job-market-for-underwater-welders/.

98. Michael Guta, "Underwater Robotics to Grow Nearly 7 Percent in Next 4 Years," *RobotXworld*, May 20, 2013, http://www.robotxworld.com/topics/robotics/articles/338714-underwater-robotics-grow-nearly-7-percent-next-4.htm.

99. IBISWorld, "Autonomous Underwater Vehicle Manufacturing in the US Industry Market Research Report Now Available from IBISWorld," news release, May 23, 2013, http://www.prweb.com/releases/2013/5/prweb10758108.htm.

100. "Global Careers in Marine Contracting," IMCA, accessed August 5, 2013, http://www.imca-int.com/careers.aspx.

101. "Make the Move," IMCA, accessed August 5, 2013, http://www.imca-int.com/careers/make-the-move.aspx.

102. "Education & Careers," ACUA, accessed August 5, 2013, http://www.acuaonline.org/education-careers.

103. Rick Suttle, "Underwater Photographer Pay Scale," *Houston Chronicle*, accessed August 5, 2013, http://work.chron.com/underwater-photographer-pay-scale-20216.html.

104. Julia Estrela, "Underwater Hotels in the Florida Keys," *eHow*, accessed August 5, 2013, http://www.ehow.com/list_6834841_underwater-hotels-florida-keys.html.

105. Kelly O'Mara, "Underwater Tourism: There's Nowhere to Go But Down," *Yahoo! Travel*, July 23, 2012, http://travel.yahoo.com/ideas/underwater-tourism--there-s-nowhere-to-go-but-down.html?page=all.

106. Ker Than, "Virgin Galactic Unveils First Tourist Spaceship," *National Geographic News*, December 8, 2009, http://news.nationalgeographic.com/news/2009/12/091208-virgin-galactic-spaceship-enterprise-branson/.

107. Carolyn Said, "Google's Brin Signs Up to Be Space Tourist," *San Francisco Chronicle*, June 12, 2008, http://www.sfgate.com/news/article/Google-s-Brin-signs-up-to-be-space-tourist-3210241.php.

108. William E. Halal, "Space Tourism—Intro. SB," *TechCast*, August 3, 2013, http://www.techcast.org/BreakthroughAnalysis.aspx?ID=76.

109. Ibid.

110. Irene Klotz, "U.S. Space Tourism Set for Takeoff by 2014, FAA Says," *Reuters*, March 21, 2012, http://www.reuters.com/article/2012/03/21/uk-usa-space-tourism-idUSLNE82K01420120321.

111. Patrick Collins and Adriano Autino, "What the Growth of a Space Tourism Industry Could Contribute to Employment, Economic Growth, Environmental Protection, Education, Culture and World Peace," *Space Future*, May 25, 2008, http://www.spacefuture.com/archive/what_the_growth_of_a_space_tourism_industry_could_contribute_to_employment_economic_growth_environmental_protection_education_culture_and_world_peace.shtml.

CHAPTER FOUR

On the Front Lines of Career Planning

HR Professionals Discuss What's New in Career Development

Few people in a company are as close to the career planning process as those in human resources. HR professionals have witnessed the shift from linear careers to portfolio careers firsthand. To learn what new trends and innovations are shaping the career development field—and how individuals can take advantage of them—we spoke with 20 HR experts and business owners representing organizations ranging from small boutique firms to startups to some of the world's largest professional service companies. Here are their insights.

Coming to a Company Near You: Career Planning Today

HR professionals have witnessed a sea change in the management of career planning. In particular, they note, both companies and individuals have become more amenable to lattice and labyrinthine career paths. "There's a much stronger focus on the winding path," says Carmen,* an HR executive at a leading pharmaceutical firm, who cites the example of an executive vice president and chief risk officer who took a job as a market president in preparation for a line role. "Someone might look at that move as a step backwards, but that woman is actually shifting her career path and aligning it with where she ultimately wants to go."

To make alternative career paths work, Nancy Sullivan, senior vice president at Lee Hecht Harrison, says, companies have to consider alternatives to promo-

* Name has been changed at the interviewee's request.

tion in order to motivate high performers. "Make horizontal movement as rewardable as upward mobility," she advises, "because you're incentivizing that key talent to stay in your company." Carmen suggests that companies make salary grades broad enough that employees don't have to take a pay cut if they make a lateral or backward move, and that firms reconsider the messages they send about growth and success.

Another exciting trend HR experts are seeing is the creation of separate career tracks for managers and technical specialists who don't want to manage others. For example, companies may opt to measure engineers' career development by milestones such as receiving patents rather than by how many people they oversee. "I consulted for a software company that was having difficulty retaining engineers," says Meg Paradise, an organizational development consultant for the 1199 National Benefit Fund. "We realized engineers were leaving because they didn't want to be managing others, so we implemented non-management career paths for them. It was a major undertaking to create senior roles that didn't include client-facing responsibilities, but the company recognized how difficult it would be to replace engineers capable of winning patents."

Specialist career tracks often include new senior positions that don't involve management. Networking appliances company F5 Networks, for example, has non-management roles called architect and evangelist. Architects, Rich James, director of global staffing at F5 Networks, explains, are roughly equivalent to directors. They're well-compensated individual contributors who are recognized subject matter experts. They may lead teams but don't always manage people. Evangelists, James says, promote the company by presenting at conferences and working on project proposals.

Many technology companies have both individual contributor and management tracks. "Some great coders are never going to be happy leading a team of people, but they still have room to grow in their role," says Christine Roggenbusch, vice president of business operations and human resources at nPario, a startup that helps companies analyze big data. At Sun Microsystems, where she formerly worked, career paths for individual contributors were couched in terms of development experiences rather than job titles.

Many companies' career development systems now focus on versatility rather than specialization, HR experts say. "People used to be rewarded for doing the same thing over and over," says Ellen,* a consultant and a former chief talent officer with 25 years' HR experience. "Now, employers believe that, if you do the same job too long, you're not learning anything. They want to see employees take on many different assignments to broaden their skill sets."

* Name has been changed at the interviewee's request.

Companies today are also offering fewer specific, structured career paths than they did in the 1980s and 90s, and fewer fast-tracking and training options for high potentials. In part, this has happened because members of younger generations don't plan to stay with any one firm for long, and companies don't want to invest heavily in employees who will leave after three or four years.

Some HR professionals, however, are seeing companies partnering with employees to map out career paths, which they view as a positive trend. "When companies stopped directing career paths, employees became the sole proprietors of their careers," says Paradise. "But if you leave it up to employees to choose which programs or resources they want to use, they develop a mindset that they're in the game alone. They think 'I can develop my career here or I can go somewhere else.' If you're collaborating with employees, though, asking them where they want to go and what they need to do to get there, you're creating a partnership with them."

Companies have also recognized that not all employees are motivated by money and prestige, and are reshaping their career development systems to reflect this shift in values. "We retain people by paying attention to what motivates them, whether it's a high salary, more educational opportunities, or more vacation time," says Rich Andersen, CEO of staffing and recruiting firm Goldstar Global. "Employees don't find top positions as attractive as they once did," says Allison,* who works for a major financial consulting firm. "People see that many senior executives don't lead balanced lives, and they'd prefer to have greater work-life balance in their own lives. Companies have responded by providing more opportunities for flexibility, such as part-time and short-term seasonal positions for skilled workers." She concludes, "The on-call, high-caliber workforce will become an integral part of managing work for many firms."

Firms are also paying greater attention to their corporate culture, partly in order to improve retention. Sam Wageman, president of Fusion Medical Staffing, believes his firm's culture is one reason his employees stay around. "Our company is committed to honesty," he says. "We value open communication, and believe that productive conflict is a good thing. When firms don't address employee concerns, resentment can simmer and spread. We're also careful to treat employees well. We value diversity and team goals, and provide profit sharing for the entire firm. Great satisfaction comes when I hear our people say they look forward to coming in to work on Mondays."

Mark,* CEO of a small firm that employees rarely leave, also thinks culture is key to retention. "To the degree that it's possible, create a stress-free work environment," he suggests. "Emphasize recognition and appreciation. Give employees the option to work remotely or have flexible work hours, and compensate them as well as the demands of your business allow."

* Name has been changed at the interviewee's request.

Firms Have a Vital Role to Play in Career Development

All the HR specialists we interviewed, in fact, agreed that firms should play a role in career development, because doing so is one way they can retain their greatest resource—talent. "To stay competitive in spite of increased competition, firms have to create nimble and highly adaptive cultures," says Barbara,* who was formerly an executive working in business development for a Silicon Valley-based coaching firm. "And the way they do that is through their people. For companies to sustain global or even local leadership, they must optimize their people through development programs."

Development is essential to maintaining a talent pipeline, says James: "Giving someone a career path they're excited about makes it less likely they'll leave—and it's easier than finding new experts to replace those who've gone." Megan Remark, senior vice president at HealthPartners, agrees. "I consider building our bench strength one of my primary jobs as an executive," she says. "Cultures only survive when you pass them on to the next generation. Your organization has a better chance of surviving when you have career development opportunities that provide continuity for your business."

Plus, career development programs contribute to employee engagement, says Sullivan. "Lack of development opportunities is one of the top three reasons employees are dissatisfied with their employers," she notes. "Firms need to have thriving, engaged workers who want to grow without leaving their companies," says Pamela Hardy, assistant vice president of organization and talent development for a major healthcare system. "I hate it when knowledge walks out the door."

"Employees, especially younger ones, won't know everything they need to know to excel at their jobs right away," says Tim Russell, manager of learning and development at a well-known technology firm. "I believe it's the company's responsibility to provide some education if they want to get the most from their employees."

How Firms Can Improve Their Career Development Systems

When asked what best practices firms should adopt to improve their career development programs, HR professionals keep coming back to one word: transparency. HR experts believe that, to advance, employees must know what's expected of them. Managers, too, they say, should be conversant with their organizations' career paths so they can help employees to find the right ones.

Competency models are one way to improve transparency and help employees set goals and identify areas for improvement. "One of my former employers, a Fortune 500 mixed-industrial company, made sure that all employees used the

---

* Name has been changed at the interviewee's request.

same leadership model," says Karen Robinson, senior director of human resources at the Apollo Group. "As a result, everyone knew how the company defined leadership and what competencies they needed to display."

Such models are an improvement upon yearly performance reviews, some HR professionals believe. "Competency plans are living and breathing," unlike yearly reviews, which are static, says Andrew Greenberg, founder and managing partner of The Recruiting Division. In fact, some firms have eliminated performance reviews altogether in favor of real-time feedback. Amy,* who was formerly a division vice president at a Fortune 500 technology services firm, says, "Younger employees, who often aren't planning on staying in any one company for long, prefer real-time feedback to yearly reviews, as it's more useful to them after they leave a firm."

Technology can be an avenue to greater transparency. Social collaborative learning systems, for example, can give all employees an equal voice and equal access to resources, while providing employers insight into their workforce. "With social collaboration, you can see who is interested, who is skilled, who is performing, and who is engaged," says Keith Meyerson, vice president of talent management and organizational strategies at Bluewater Learning, a consulting firm that specializes in learning and talent development. "Employees can use it to let the organization know about their skills and interests and to connect with others who can mentor them or guide them to the career path they want."

Firms should also cultivate a mentoring culture, HR experts believe. "People typically do the things that are rewarded," says Meyerson. "If learning and development is important, than that needs to be weighted in performance reviews. If your first line supervisors don't understand the importance of having a collaborative coaching environment, you'll have a hard time encouraging internal growth."

Coach high performers, not just the people in trouble, says Remark: "Spend the money on the people you want to retain, not those you must discipline." In her company, for example, people identified as potential leaders, especially physicians who may not have much administrative experience, may receive one or two years of executive coaching to prepare them for new roles.

Integrate career development and performance management, Carmen suggests. "Make both performance management and career pathing an ongoing dialogue between managers and employees," she says. "Managers should discuss not only what an employee needs to do to fill performance gaps for her current job, but also what she needs to do to prepare for her next role."

Managers are crucial to the career development process, our HR experts say, but note that their role is often overlooked. "Managers need to be rewarded and evaluated on their contributions to the talent development process," says Russell. "Their workload needs to be balanced so that they're not expected to achieve

* Name has been changed at the interviewee's request.

the same results as an individual contributor. They should be attaining results through other people." Executives, too, should be rewarded for their contributions to employee development, says Amy, who notes that executives often work to develop employees without being compensated for it.

Finally, HR professionals stress that career development starts with hiring the right people. To onboard talent that's a good fit, companies first need to define their corporate culture. "If your culture is warm, friendly, and collaborative, you don't want to hire sharks who'll be fighting for sales," says Meyerson. "Everyone who's hiring needs to understand the culture so you can onboard people who'll be able to adopt the rites and rituals of your organization."

"My company hires for cultural fit even before we hire for technical expertise," says Russell. "To work for us, you need to be humble and know that arrogance and ego don't work here. In that way, we preserve the DNA of our culture."

Best Practices for Career Development: For Employers

"Implement leader-to-leader sharing through technologies such as Skype and WebEx." —Barbara

"Expect that employees will and should move around within your firm. Have an internal job board to facilitate movement within your company." —Amy

"Set up rotation programs between small and large firms so employees can get to know the culture and processes of each. New experiences can spark innovation." —Roggenbusch

"Have honest conversations with employees about whether or not they're being considered for leadership roles so they can plan their careers accordingly. They've invested a lot of time with your company and deserve honesty. If they know they don't have much room for advancement at your firm and want to move on, help to place them with clients or customers." —Allison

"Partner with educators. Some companies, for example, offer on-site executive MBA programs as part of their development plan for high potentials." —Hardy

"Host entrepreneurial competitions during which groups of employees present ideas for new products or business services. Reward the winners by funding their ideas." —Amy

"Provide 360-degree feedback for all employees, not just the executives." —Ellen

"Hold performance conversations quarterly, not annually. Millennials in particular prefer more frequent feedback." —Sullivan

"New blood offers new things. If you're only building talent and not buying talent, that's a problem." —Russell

"Create career maps that tell employees what competencies they need to have to be successful in a given role, and what they need to do to advance to different roles." —Robinson

"Post your career architecture online so everyone knows what it takes to get to the top." —Ellen

"Allow development packages to be customized for different employees." —Robinson

"Assign high potentials special projects that give them insight into what the next level of their career could look like." —Remark

"Have employees prepare comprehensive personal career development plans with support from management, on work time." —Allison

"Keep in touch with high potentials when they leave. We've found that many of ours come back with refreshed perspectives and renewed energy." —Sara Lautenbach, director of diversity and talent acquisition at Sutter Health

"Consider Management by Objective: evaluating individuals and teams by their accomplishments, not by the amount of face time they've put in. This type of management bases rewards on merit and helps facilitate virtual and face-to-face collaboration." —Amy

"Integrate performance management processes with development processes. Career development shouldn't be arbitrary; it should be tied to performance and whether someone meets expectations." —Russell

"Pre-hiring assessments let you create development plans that individuals can use from the day they come on board to the day they leave the company." —Hardy

"Implement a structured rewards program which ties rewards to job descriptions or company values. These rewards can be something as simple as a gift certificate or elaborate as a vacation for two to an exotic destination." —James

"Pair high performers with mentors who aren't in their chain of command so they can feel safe speaking to them openly." —Remark

How Individuals Can Boost Their Career Development

HR professionals agree that, today, individuals need to take charge of their own career planning and not just passively let their careers happen. "You can't just sit there and make the widget every day. If you want to be considered for positions, you have to put yourself out there," says Meyerson, who lists taking competency assessments and completing information in talent management systems as two ways employees can do so. "The thing that most differentiates high potentials from others is that they don't wait for the organization to teach them something," he adds. "If there's something they don't know how to do, they'll go out and learn it on their own."

Showing initiative is vital, Katherine Markgraf, Assistant Director of Executive Recruiting, Tax at Ernst & Young, believes.[*] "Employers like people who are overachievers and have examples to prove it—people who can point to errors they corrected or revenue opportunities they identified," she says. "I've found that if people showed initiative in the past they'll likely do so again."

"Firms are looking for people who are proactive about self-education, skill development, and finding growth opportunities for their companies," says Amy. "They're less interested in training employees to become executives; they'd rather hire someone who can contribute starting on day one."

Have a career plan, even if you don't want to be promoted, HR professionals recommend. "Whether you're upwardly mobile or want to make a lateral move,

---

Best Practices for Planning Your Career

"Take advantage of whatever free resources your firm offers." —Greenberg

"Never speak negatively behind someone's back. Respect is key." —Barbara

"Take advantage of both internal and external expert training. If you're an accounting professional, for example, you can take classes offered by CPA societies." —Markgraf

"Be a servant leader. Support your colleagues and your department rather than yourself. Team effort is rewarded." —Meyerson

"Seek feedback from your manager and peers, especially if you work for a company without a highly structured career development process." —Ellen

"Create a personal mission statement and put it on your screen saver or your desk." —Markgraf

"Join professional organizations to stay up-to-date with trends in your industry." —Robinson

"Be forward-thinking. Ask yourself what will be important to your organization five years down the road. Don't become a dinosaur." —Meyerson

"Serve your community as a volunteer or board member for a charity. Employers have become more global and socially conscious and they want their employees to reflect their values." —Markgraf

"Hold informational interviews with people inside and outside your firm to learn what is required to attain different positions." —Amy

---

[*] Interviewee requested that her title be capitalized.

"Go on a personal retreat: Take a day off and spend some quiet time thinking about your career and where you want to go." —Andersen

"Read the annual reports to better understand what your organization values." —Greenberg

"Find a personal cheerleader: someone who'll promote you even when you're not in the room." —Markgraf

"Gain both line and staff experience." —Lautenbach

"Develop relationships with the people who are involved in employee development. HR is a good place to start." —Greenberg

"If you don't have a good manager, get one." —Russell

"Learn your strengths and weaknesses through mentoring, coaching, or formal 360-degree feedback. Be open to constructive criticism." —Carmen

"Become the go-to person in your subject area and people will seek you out." —Markgraf

"Don't assume you'll stay with any one company for long. Use your time at a firm to acquire the skills and experiences you'll need to make your next move." —Amy

"Be open to relocating. It exponentially expands your opportunities." —Carmen

"Learn where the opportunities for development are. Talk to people who have the role you want to move into." —Robinson

"Focus on your strengths, not your weaknesses. Rather than trying to improve your weakest areas, choose roles or career paths that play to your strengths." —Russell

"Be available for special projects that fall outside your job description." —Markgraf

"Find a mentor or sponsor in the senior levels of your company who can bring your name up at C-level meetings. If you're not known at the upper levels you'll have a harder time being promoted." —Paradise

decelerate, or stay where you are, you need a plan," Sullivan says. "Regardless of your career goals, make a plan and discuss it regularly with your manager."

"View yourself as an entrepreneur," says Andersen. "Create a personal business plan for your career, and be proactive about managing your growth within your company to reach your goals."

Let your superiors know about your career plan, suggests Remark. "Keep them informed about the skills you want to obtain and the new experiences you want to be exposed to," she says. "They can direct you to classes and training, shadowing opportunities, or new projects."

Many HR professionals recommend broadening your range of experiences. "Take part in special initiatives, in things that get you out of your day job," says Carmen. "That's how you expose yourself to new subject matter and to different parts of the organization. You lay the foundation for being given opportunities by expanding your network and getting to know people who otherwise wouldn't know who you are."

"Employers value breadth of experience," adds Robinson. "They like seeing expertise in many functions."

Learning agility is a vital skill to cultivate, says Carmen: "The ability to move up the learning curve quickly and to apply your skills and knowledge effectively in new situations is very important."

The Future of Career Development

Our interviewees see many exciting changes ahead in the world of career development. In particular, they believe technology has the potential to reshape the field. Training and development has advanced along with technology, Meyerson says, moving from instructor-led training to e-learning, or computer-enhanced learning using networked and/or multimedia technologies, such as Internet-based classes or classes which incorporate video, CD-ROMs, online or computer games, and other such methods.[1] When mobile devices became widespread, companies began using m-learning, or mobile learning: learning enabled by the use of smartphones, tablets, MP3 players, and other portable devices.[2] Now, s-learning, or social learning—learning that takes place over social media—is the latest technology to impact the learning and development field.

"S-learning is the newest and most important delivery method we've seen to date," says Meyerson, who believes that collaborative social learning systems show great promise. "They democratize access to information," she says. "The people who are closest to problems can provide solutions, regardless of their position in the company's hierarchy."

Another advantage of social learning systems is that they allow for just-in-time learning. "These days, when people want to learn something, they don't wait to take a class to do so," says Russell. "They perform a quick Internet search and figure it out right away. The future of learning is not so much about content creation as it is about content management: organizing knowledge efficiently so people can learn in real time on the job."

New technologies can also make it easier to retain employees. "We're implementing systems that will make it easier for people to identify jobs within our organization, much like an internal CareerBuilder or LinkedIn," says Carmen.

"When employees are looking for new jobs, they can find opportunities without leaving the company."

As useful as new technologies have been, companies are beginning to realize there are some things you can't do over the Internet. "At my company, we're always communicating with our parent company in Asia," says Russell. "And we've found that you can do more in one visit overseas where you're interacting face-to-face with your peers than you can in weeks on the phone."

Russell believes the learning and development sector is coming to the same conclusion. "For a while, most of the key players in the learning and development world were advocating virtual learning and online social collaboration," he relates. "I recently attended a chief learning officers' symposium, and we were discussing how the pendulum is swinging back the other direction, that, for some subjects, getting people into a physical classroom can accomplish more than e-learning."

Companies are also thinking creatively about how to improve their talent pipelines, HR professionals say. One key way they do so is by working with educators. "HealthPartners provides residencies where interns are paired with senior leaders and get a bird's-eye view of different aspects of their jobs," says Remark. "They experience a variety of different roles and responsibilities ranging from operations to staff management to strategic planning, which gives them an idea of the kind of career they might want to pursue. That program's been a source of new employees."

HealthPartners also reaches out to universities. "It's a way of exposing large groups of people to our organization, people who may find that our mission and values resonate with them," Remark says. "I've met many diverse candidates by speaking at master programs on campus."

Some companies start laying the groundwork for employment pipelines even earlier than college. Sullivan worked with an engineering firm that gave talks at high schools to encourage students to pursue science and engineering careers. "That company's leaders looked far beyond their four walls to develop talent," she says.

Other companies are behaving in a way that, at first glance, seems counterintuitive: Rather than focusing on retaining talent, they're acknowledging that employees won't stay with them long, and designing their development structures around that fact. "Today, people spend two to five years with an organization rather than five to 10," says Robinson. "Companies need to focus on shorter-term development opportunities, quick wins that allow employees to experience career acceleration. For example, they can arrange for recent graduates to have career movement in their first year with an organization. That keeps people engaged and can increase their tenure with an organization." Allison agrees: "Companies can cut time to promotion by helping top performers develop career plans that include team projects, progression charts, and personal branding efforts."

Meyerson predicts that, in years to come, employees and organizations will find themselves on a more equal footing. "Employees and employers will act more like partners," he says. "The old-school mentality that workers need to conform to the company's standards is outdated. Workers are the new consumers, and just as businesses change their tactics to meet consumer demand, companies will need to change their policies to attract the best talent."

Innovations in Career Development

"Some companies offer day- or week-long internal internships that allow employees to shadow colleagues with very different roles." —Amy

"At W.L. Gore and Associates, most units have a maximum of 200 employees. That small size allows for a great deal of flexibility. People perform job rotations where they have short stints in different roles." —Russell

"North Virginia Family Services helps people who want to re-enter the workforce. The organization has put together career maps that let people know the exact education and certifications they need to go from housekeeping or food services to clinical healthcare positions. This program is aimed at the immigrant population but it's an idea that could work for everyone." —Hardy

"One of my previous employers, a Fortune 100 engineering company, takes a scientific approach to career development. The company uses predictive modeling to assess the characteristics of high potentials early in their career and uses the results to accelerate their development." —Robinson

"Some firms have introduced a position called retention manager: a designated HR professional in charge of retention." —Greenberg

"Learning and development used to focus on creating well-rounded employees. But according to the Strengths Model, a new approach to learning and development, it's better to hire for diversity and passion and then maximize each employee's strengths." —Russell

"Some companies have internal cohort education programs in which senior executives and subject matter experts work together on case studies based on their firms' real-life challenges. Learning that is tied to the real world can make education feel more practical and relevant." —Amy

"Yahoo! uses internal social media to help employees develop mentoring relationships." —Roggenbusch

"Some firms provide case studies for college students to work on, which give them a feel for what it's like to work in a given industry. It's like an internship before the internship." —Allison

Other innovations from leading companies:

- Facebook puts all its new engineers through a "boot camp" where they start learning the company's massive codebase, solve problems as a group, and explore different areas of the firm to see where they might best fit. Facebook also allows its developers to periodically take a month off from their roles to try out different jobs and areas of the company by working on new projects with other teams.[3]

- One of Google's hiring managers reads resumes from the bottom up because people's hobbies, volunteer work, and early work experiences give him better insight into whether they'll fit into Google's culture than their more recent experience.[4]

- Some companies are using alternatives to the resume, such as examining candidates' social media presence and video profiles, to determine whether job applicants would make suitable employees.[5]

- At Whole Foods, most major decisions, including those pertaining to staffing and strategy, are made by consensus. Employees at all levels can participate in the hiring of both coworkers and senior executives.[6]

- PepsiCo provides its employees with opportunities for stretch assignments, job rotations, responsibility in early career, and mentoring. Eighty percent of its executive team was promoted from within.[7]

- Medical staffing firm CHG Healthcare Services gives sales teams paid time off for meeting their goals.[8]

- Ultimate Software pays all healthcare premiums for its employees and their dependents and gives employees a free vacation every two years.[9]

Notes

1. *Wikipedia*, s.v., "E-learning," last modified July 26, 2013, http://en.wikipedia.org/wiki/E_ learning; Tracey Wilen-Daugenti, *.edu: Technology and Learning Environments in Higher Education* (New York: Peter Lang, 2009), 183.
2. *Wikipedia*, s.v., "M-learning," last modified June 15, 2013, http://en.wikipedia.org/wiki/M-learning; Wilen-Daugenti, *.edu: Technology and Learning Environments*, 185.
3. Jolie O'Dell, "Bootcamp! How Facebook Indoctrinates Every New Engineer It Hires," *VentureBeat*, March 2, 2013, http://venturebeat.com/2013/03/02/facebook-bootcamp/.
4. Derek Loosvelt, "Do You Fit Into Google's Culture?," *Vault*, January 25, 2012, http://blogs.vault.com/blog/resumes-cover-letters/do-you-fit-into-googles-culture/.
5. Ibid.
6. Jessica Rohman, "Higher Purpose, Shared Fate," *Great Place to Work*, March 6, 2013, http://www.greatplacetowork.com/publications-and-events/blogs-and-news/1648-whole-foods.
7. "Real World Leadership," PepsiCo.com, accessed July 27, 2013, http://www.pepsico.com/Careers/Why-Work-at-PepsiCo/Training-and-Development.html.

8. "100 Best Companies to Work For," *Fortune*, February 4, 2013, http://money.cnn.com/magazines/fortune/best-companies/2013/snapshots/3.html?iid=bc_sp_list.

9. Ibid.

CHAPTER FIVE

Recruiters Speak

Skills to Have, Trends to Know About, and Tips for Job-Hunting Success

If you want to know what today's employers are looking for, you'd do well to ask a recruiter. Recruiters are the professionals companies rely upon to locate top talent for their most challenging and best-compensated positions. As a result, recruiters have an insider's perspective on what jobs and skills are most in demand, what job-hunting practices are most effective, and what it takes to capture an employer's attention.

We interviewed 15 recruiters specializing in sectors ranging from technology to finance to healthcare, asking them what job seekers need to know to succeed on today's job market. Here's their advice.

Recruiting Today: Technology Brings Convenience and Competition

Technology, recruiters agree, has permanently changed the employment landscape for both recruiting firms and job seekers—so it's critical that job hunters know how to maximize its potential. The Internet has made it possible for recruiters to reach more candidates more quickly than ever before, and for job hunters to research companies and find open positions. Social media, in particular, has become an integral part of the recruiting and job seeking process.

"Before the Internet, the only way to find candidates was to cold call," says Andrew Greenberg, founder and managing partner of The Recruiting Division, a firm offering on-demand talent recruitment. "When the Internet became mainstream, recruiters used job boards. Now, we're in the social media era." Around 85% of all positions, some recruiters say, are filled through networking and LinkedIn.

"LinkedIn has made it easier to find qualified people because it lets recruiters search profiles for specialized skill sets," says Jennifer Brent, a senior recruiter specializing in banking, marketing, and technology at Gent & Associates. "If I post an opening to a job board the quality of resumes I receive can be terrible. People will reply without having any qualifications. Solid candidates aren't using job boards: They're networking or are on LinkedIn."

Social media has helped shift the balance of power towards job seekers. "In the recruiting world today, there's much more emphasis on candidate care, partly because candidates are sharing their experiences on social media," says Greenberg. "If they post about having a great experience in the interview process, it can go viral, which will help the firm and the recruiter."

At the same time, though, technology has increased competition for talent and for jobs. Hiring managers and recruiters are now swamped with resumes, and candidates are finding it harder to compete against so many other job seekers. "Today, those who get hired are the best of the best," says Lisa Francone, a recruiter specializing in technology at Gent & Associates. "In the past, you needed to fulfill 50% of the requirements listed in a job posting. Now, you need to fulfill 100% and more."

Technology has also made recruiters' jobs more complex. "There used to be one or two job boards for the types of nurses we target," says Rich Smith, managing partner at nursing staffing agency Atlas MedStaff. "Now there are hundreds." Ironically, having more ways to contact people has made them harder to reach, says Maureen Perkins, a recruiter specializing in technology and engineering at Gent & Associates: "When all we had to rely on were phone calls and face-to-face interviews, people were more responsive."

Smith expects that recruiters will become more dependent on mobile technology in the near future. "Job hunters want to be able to apply for a job on their iPhone, schedule an interview via text, and accept the position on the spot," he says. "The instant they step out of the hiring manager's office they'll post their excitement about their new job on Facebook and link it back to the company page."

Yet some things haven't changed. Despite having new ways to reach out to talent, companies will always need recruiters for the human element they provide, says Leslie Lazarus, a senior recruiter specializing in finance, accounting, retail, and HR at Gent & Associates. "There's only so much technology can do," she notes. "Recruiters are able to see the human aspects in a resume or LinkedIn profile."

"Recruiters can attest to a candidate's personality and soft skills and what references had to say about him, things that aren't visible on a resume," says Sheila

Maultsby, staffing manager at Accountemps, a division of Robert Half International.

And, even in an age of high technology, candidates still need classic job hunting skills. "It's challenging to stand out against the 'noise' of so many applicants," says Anne Angelopoulos, senior manager specializing in human resources, contract recruiting, and temporary staffing at national staffing firm Juststaff. "In that regard, the old-fashioned practices of persistence, networking, negotiating, and professionalism are still so critical."

Skill Requirements in an Employer's Market

Recruiters—and job hunters—must keep a close eye on the economy, which drives employment trends. As Gary Daugenti explains, "When the unemployment rate is high, it's an employer's market, and when the unemployment rate is low, it's an employee's market. The dotcom bubble of the late 90s, for instance, was the epitome of an employee's market. The national unemployment rate was down to 4.5%, the stock market was at an all-time high, and money from venture capital was flowing like a broken fire hydrant. Candidates were literally doubling their salaries overnight, landing VP titles with little or no management experience, and acquiring significant equity in some companies. When the bubble popped, many of these same candidates had to face the reality that their qualifications did not match the salaries and titles they had gained, and had to settle for lower positions and less compensation."

The mortgage crisis of 2008, on the other hand, created an employer's market, with companies having their pick of top talent in many fields. In such a market, employers can afford to be highly selective. "In the past, companies looking to hire technology professionals just wanted those with the right technology skill sets," says Francone. "Now, they require communications, management, and team building skills in addition to technological proficiency."

Many companies require industry-specific experience, especially for senior positions. "Firms today have exacting requirements," says Maureen Perkins. "For example, a bicycle company with an opening for a mechanical engineer won't hire a mechanical engineer from the dental industry—they want someone with bicycle experience." Having direct industry experience, says Carolyn Redman, a senior recruiter specializing in sales and operations at SearchFirst Group, enables an employee to perform at a high level from day one, something companies desire. "They're not as willing to train candidates," she says.

Recruiters are also seeing less urgency to hire. "In the late 1990s, companies made quick hiring decisions without putting candidates through the technical testing or thorough interview processes they have now," Francone recalls. "Candidates also research prospective employers more thoroughly before they accept positions. The matches made now are very solid."

"The hiring process takes much longer than it used to—up to two months," says Brent. "Firms can require up to seven interviews. They're also more cautious about hiring as they're hoping to take on people who will stay with them for four or five years, not 18 months."

However, there are some indications that the market is beginning to change. "I've found that candidates are now getting multiple offers and are rejecting jobs that don't appeal to them more than they did a few years ago," Daugenti says.

Cultural Fit Is Now a Factor

Companies are also placing more emphasis on cultural fit when hiring, recruiters say. "Employers want candidates who'll fit in with their culture and perform well from day one," says Perkins. "For example, a smaller firm might be reluctant to hire someone who'd only worked for Fortune 100 companies out of concern that that person wouldn't be able to adapt to the tight budgets and all-hands-on-deck mentality small firms have."

Employees, especially highly sought-after candidates with technological skills, are also considering how well a company's culture suits them. "Technology employees have experienced being treated like commodities during the recession,

---

Hiring Trends by Industry

Technology:

"In the early 2000s, developers were treated like commodities, and a lot of development work went overseas. Due to language and cultural differences, that didn't always work out. Today, developers are viewed as vital employees who enrich their firms, and they're in high demand." —Greenberg

"There tends to be a good deal of turnover in IT. Technology employees consider continual learning part of the value they bring to a firm, and if they're not provided with the most up-to-date technology they'll move on." —Perkins

Sales:

"Sales candidates are still more concerned about salary than lifestyle or cultural fit. They're doing more homework about companies and considering industry trends and new technologies when deciding whether to take a job." —Greenberg

"Companies are looking for MBAs, not just bachelor's degrees." —Redman

HR and Marketing:

"These areas are becoming more project-oriented. Rather than bringing in permanent employees, companies are hiring contractors to complete large projects. There's a real reluctance to commit to increasing payroll during these uncertain times." —Angelopoulos

HR:

"Companies are breaking down their HR departments by function: for example, having one HR division oversee sales and finance and a different one oversee IT. Firms are looking to hire specialists such as directors of benefits and compensation, training and development, or diversity." —Lazarus

Marketing:

"Companies are looking for people with experience in social media marketing and digital commerce. They're not as interested in traditional marketing experience any more." —Brent

Nursing:

"Highly specialized nurses are in demand, but they tend to be so well-paid that they're not willing to change employers. There's also increased demand for basic home health RNs. New nurses now have more job options outside the hospital setting." —Smith

Finance:

"Regardless of your role, employers expect you to have a bachelor's degree in accounting or finance, excellent communication skills, interpersonal skills, advanced Microsoft Excel skills, and a flexible attitude." —Maultsby

"There's great demand for people who understand the US government's compliance regulations or international compliance regulations." —Brent

"Companies are placing a lot of emphasis on lean principles and Six Sigma." —Lazarus

"In the tax arena, companies are looking for CPAs and people who can move into operations." —Lazarus

IT Sales:

"Companies want people who have worked for well-known companies, but people with jobs at brand name firms tend to not want to leave." —Redman

and they don't want to repeat that experience," says Greenberg. "They now consider lifestyle and corporate culture when deciding whether to accept a job offer."

Best Practices for Job Seekers

Recruiters talk to job seekers day in, day out. From setting career goals to perfecting your resume, from using technology to networking, they know what works and what doesn't. Here, they share some of their best practices for finding a job that's right for you.

Every job search starts with goals, says Jim Stroud, director of sourcing and social strategy at Bernard Hodes Group and author of *Resume Forensics: How to Find Free Resumes and Passive Candidates on Google*: "Figure out who you want

Where the Jobs Are

Recruiters expect hiring to remain brisk in these fields:

- STEM (science, technology, engineering, and mathematics), especially information technology and biotechnology
- Healthcare
- Nursing
- Physical and occupational therapy
- Lab technicians
- Biotechnology
- Sales
- Technical marketing and sales
- Business development
- Corporate tax
- Quality assurance

Recruiters name these positions as their hardest to fill:

- Global vice presidents
- Specialized engineers, especially chemical, metallurgical, and oil and gas
- Specialized nurses, especially those specializing in pediatric and neonatal intensive care, cardiovascular nursing, and catheterization lab nursing
- Physical and occupational therapists
- People willing to take jobs in rural or less desirable locations
- Women for key roles in finance
- Mobile, especially Android, and Java developers
- Software architecture roles
- Analysts, especially senior financial analysts

to be when you grow up. There is no way you can go from point A to point B without a reference point."

If you don't have a dream vocation in mind, Stroud suggests doing some research and determining which jobs will be hot in the future. "Consider 3-D printing, for example, which is something which could have a profound effect on the global economy," he says. "If people start printing clothes with a 3-D printer, many clothing retailers and manufacturers could go out of business." But, he points out, other jobs would be created designing and repairing 3-D printers and designing items for others to print. The Bureau of Labor Statistics' Occupational

Outlook, Stroud says, is a helpful resource for determining how popular certain jobs will be over the next decade.

Finding the right role models can be helpful, Stroud says. "Search LinkedIn for people who are doing what you'd like to be doing, and study everything they did prior to arriving where they are now," he suggests. "Also, consider reaching out to them and asking for their mentorship."

Having the right attitude is important, say recruiters, as is being flexible. Our recruiters report there are many more job openings in less prominent areas. "There's great demand for talent from small or medium-sized firms in small towns and rural areas," says Perkins. "If you're flexible about your title, salary, and location many more doors will open for you," says Angelopoulous.

It's vital to have a strong online presence and market yourself well, recruiters say. "Recruiters always look for the best candidates, but 'best' is relative," Stroud advises. "You may be more qualified than the next guy, but if you don't market yourself better than your competitors do, how will anyone know?"

"If you want to be found, leave traces online," says Vanessa,* a technical recruiter for a well-known technology firm. "My company looks for candidates on such sites as LinkedIn, Github, Talentbin, Meetup, Facebook, Google Plus, and alumni websites." Even Twitter can be a search tool, says Greenberg, who observes that some recruiters tweet the skill sets they're looking for.

LinkedIn is "the king of social media, as far as recruiting goes," says Greenberg. "Complete your LinkedIn profile," he suggests. "Join LinkedIn groups related to your industry or your area of expertise."

"Engineering and IT candidates are inundated with offers on LinkedIn," says Perkins. "Some even state on their profile, 'Please don't contact me. I'm not looking for a job.'"

Don't let the casual nature of electronic communications affect your attention to detail, cautions Elsa Meyer, a talent acquisition manager at Atlas MedStaff. "Candidates sometimes forget that anyone can be a gateway to their next employer," she says. "When emailing or texting recruiters, always show a high level of professionalism. For example, remember to add salutations."

Having a sterling resume, recruiters agree, is essential. "Recruiters receive hundreds of resumes for each position, so make sure yours stands out," says Kyle Misiak, a senior recruiter specializing in engineering, manufacturing, operations, quality, and technical sales at CSI Staffing. "Recruiters spend as little as 10 seconds scanning a resume," says Francone. "If I don't see an exact match for the job criteria I'm looking for I move on."

"Your resume should list your accomplishments, not your tasks," says Brent. "Use metrics, such as dollar amounts or percentages, to express your results. Give tangible examples of how you improved the companies you worked for."

---

* Name has been changed at the interviewee's request.

"Your resume has to be spectacular, with solid skills and no gaps," says Francone. "Make sure it includes the top keywords and SEO search terms." One way to find keywords, says Stroud, is by using LinkedIn's Skills page to determine what the popular buzzwords are in your industry. "Add these keywords to your LinkedIn profile and resume if you're honestly able to do so," says Stroud. "This can help employers and people in your field find you and connect with you."

"Don't send out a one-size-fits-all resume," advises Vanessa. "Take the time to highlight the skill sets that pertain to the job you're applying to."

Heed the classic advice to network, recruiters say, as that's a major way people find jobs. They suggesting joining groups related to your industry, attending networking events, and staying in touch with your contacts. "Make sure that you're also a good contact," says Angelopoulos. "Help bring other people together."

"Contribute to forums such as LinkedIn groups focused on your industry, and leave comments on industry blogs," says Stroud. "That way, you'll leave a trail for recruiters to follow when they Google your name." Just as having negative information linked to your name can limit your opportunities, as Stroud points out, "positive and professional commentary reflects well on you."

"Use your entire social network—every touch point, no matter how unlikely," says Greenberg. "Talk to cashiers. Talk to anyone. You never know who'll have a connection to a job."

Before an interview, do your homework, says Francone: "Research the firm and reach out to others in the company who may know the hiring manager."

But don't let a good interview make you overconfident, says Redman. "Even if an interview goes really well, remember that the position could still be put on hold or filled by an internal candidate," she says. "Keep going to interviews until you have an offer in hand."

Learn from Successful Job Hunters

To determine what job hunting practices are most and least effective today, in the spring of 2013 recruiting firm Juststaff performed a survey of 48 people who had found jobs in the past year. The results? Classic job-seeking strategies may still be the best.

The fastest path to a new job, according to the survey, is to:

- Look for a job in the same or similar industry as your previous employer.

- Look for a job in the same or similar functional area as your previous job.

- Remain active while job hunting: freelance, volunteer, or develop skills.

- Network: join industry groups, use social media, or seek job leads from people already in your network.

Thirty-five percent of respondents said they found their most recent job through networking—the most commonly given answer (see Figure 5.1). Twenty-one percent said a recruiter contacted them through social media, and 13% found their jobs on the job boards.

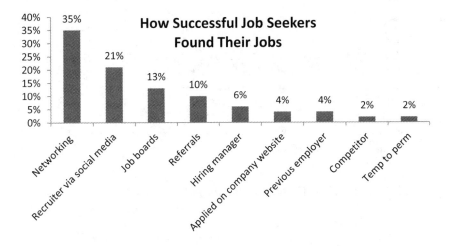

Figure 5.1. Source: Tracey Wilen-Daugenti, *Juststaff Pulse Survey Report* (Palo Alto, CA: Juststaff, 2013), 3, http://traceywilen.com/JustStaff_Pulse_Survey_Report.pdf.

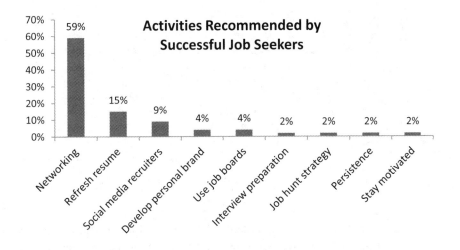

Figure 5.2. Source: Wilen-Daugenti, *Juststaff Pulse Survey Report*, 6.

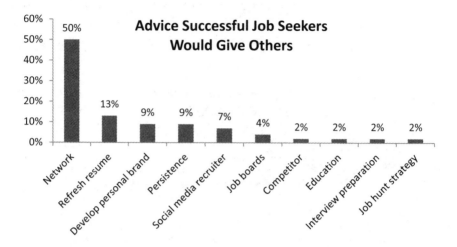

Figure 5.3. Source: Wilen-Daugenti, *Juststaff Pulse Survey Report*, 7.

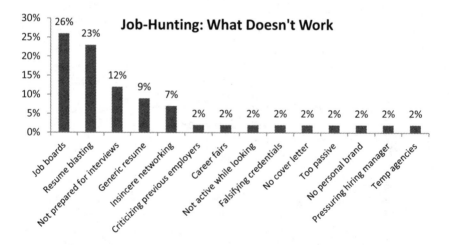

Figure 5.4. Source: Wilen-Daugenti, *Juststaff Pulse Survey Report*, 7.

Not surprisingly, 59% of respondents chose networking as the job seeking strategy they'd most recommend to others (see Figure 5.2). Fifteen percent said they'd most recommend refreshing one's resume, while 9% recommended reaching out to recruiters on social media.

When asked what advice they'd give job seekers, networking was once again the most popular choice, with 37% of respondents saying networking would be the tactic they'd be most likely to recommend (see Figure 5.3). Twenty-two percent said they'd advise others to develop a personal brand, while 15% advised applying to jobs that aligned with one's background, and 13% recommended staying motivated.

Respondents were also asked what job hunting strategies did *not* work for them. Twenty-six percent named using job boards, while 23% named resume blasting (see Figure 5.4). Twelve percent chose not being prepared for interviews as the practice they'd most avoid, while 9% chose having a generic resume.

Job-Hunting Strategies for Recent College Graduates

It can be difficult to land a job straight out of college, especially if you don't have much work experience. Daugenti advises recent graduates to start their job search by networking with hiring managers who are fellow alumni. "School ties are the perfect icebreaker," he says, "and everyone likes to hire someone they have something in common with." To find alumni who work at companies you're interested in, Daugenti suggests searching LinkedIn and contacting your alumni association.

Another strategy that Daugenti recommends is offering employers a short-term internship or a 30-day "free" trial. "Even if employers don't choose to take you up on this offer, making the offer demonstrates your creativity and eagerness to work and gives you a competitive edge over other candidates," he says.

Job-Hunting Strategies for People Over 50

For older job seekers, who may face age discrimination on the job market, Daugenti suggests a resume overhaul. "Most age bias happens before you even walk in the door," he says. "If you're over 50, you'll have a long work history. Don't advertise that fact on your resume. Only include the last 20 years of your work history and eliminate graduation dates. If you've earned an advanced degree within the last 10 to 15 years, include that information and omit your undergraduate degree."

Daugenti reminds job hunters that "the main purpose of a resume, whether you're young or old, is to get your foot in the door." In his experience, he says, "meeting someone in person eliminates about 50% of whatever age bias exists, because once you talk with them face-to-face you become a person and not just a keyword on a resume."

Daugenti suggests that older job seekers assess the age range of employees at companies they're interested in by checking out personnel photos on company webpages. "Target age-friendly companies, but don't rule out any firm that you really want to work for," he says.

When Your Search Isn't Going as Well as You'd Like

Job hunting can be a long and frustrating process. One of the most challenging aspects of looking for a job is applying for many positions and not hearing anything back from employers. In fact, 57% of people who took the Juststaff survey named not getting a response as the single most frustrating thing about job hunting—by far the most commonly selected answer.

Keep in mind, though, that not getting a response doesn't necessarily mean you're not a good candidate. "There's one simple reason most job seekers don't hear back from recruiters or companies they've applied to: bandwidth," says Daugenti. It's typical, he says, for HR professionals to receive anywhere from 30 to 200 applications for a job opening, while recruiters may work on anywhere from 10 to 40 job openings at a time, and can be managing from 200 to 1,500 replies to their openings.

Plus, Daugenti notes, some job seekers have developed a bad habit of "resume spamming" or "resume blasting": applying to a multitude of jobs they're not remotely qualified for in hopes of landing an interview through sheer luck. This practice only adds to the volume of applications HR personnel and recruiters must review. "There simply aren't enough hours in the work week for HR staff to reply to everyone who applies," Daugenti says. "And that goes double for recruiters, most of whom are paid by performance and must maximize their time on the job."

Daugenti advises job seekers not to give in to the temptation to resume spam, which is rarely effective anyway, or to apply to jobs they're not really qualified for. "I've had many candidates tell me about jobs they failed to get because they lacked the majority of the qualifications the employer was seeking," he says. "'But I'm a fast learner,' they tell me. That may be true, but remember, managers are judged by the performance of the people they hire. Just think about what kind of trouble a hiring manager could get into if he or she hired someone without the experience necessary to do a job."

Expect your job search to take plenty of time and effort, recruiters say. "Searching for a job is like a job in itself," says Greenberg. "People don't realize how much work it is." He advises organizing your search well and keeping careful records. "I'm shocked by how many job seekers don't track their contacts and activity and the jobs they apply to," he says. "Don't get frustrated," counsels Brent. "It's a long process."

CHAPTER SIX

Recruiters 101

What You Need to Know to Make Recruiters Part of Your Career Strategy

BY GARY DAUGENTI,
FOUNDER AND PRESIDENT, GENT & ASSOCIATES

Technology has dramatically changed the way that companies hire and individuals conduct their job searches. Innovations in job search tools such as social networking sites, job search engines, resume and cover letter software, and online skill assessment tools have expanded the options that job seekers have to pursue openings. The technologies employers use to find candidates have evolved as well. Applicant tracking systems, online screening tools, digital testing, and sophisticated background checking services all help employers target the best talent.

And yet finding the right person for a high level job is still an extremely complex job—all the more so today, when companies can source talent from across the country and around the world. Plus, there are some intangible aspects of the talent search process that computers just can't handle. This is where recruiters come in.

Most job seekers know all about networking, searching for open positions online, and posting their resumes to job boards. But there's one way of finding a job that's still a mystery to many: working with a recruiter. Many people don't know how or whether to contact recruiters, or what to do if a recruiter gets in touch with them. Others approach recruiters the wrong way, which hurts their chances of finding a job through a recruiter.

To successfully work with recruiters, it helps to know a little bit about what their goals are and how they function. Below, I'll explain how recruiters assess candidates, what to do if one contacts you, some best practices for working with recruiters, and some key mistakes to avoid.

Understanding Recruiters

Just as professional sports teams want to draft the best athletes, companies want to hire the best available talent. When they're serious about hiring the top employees in their industry, companies turn to recruiters.

There are three types of recruiters: agency recruiters, corporate recruiters, and contract recruiters. If a recruiter contacts you, it's fine to ask him what type of recruiter he is.

Agency recruiters, the type of recruiter most people are familiar with, are third-party vendors hired by employers. There are three subcategories of agency recruiters: contingency, temp/temp-to-perm, and retained.

Contingency recruiters are only paid upon successful hires. Their fee is typically 20% to 33% of a new hire's starting base salary or total compensation. Though that fee sounds substantial, contingency recruiters need to charge this much to stay in business, as the contingency search field is competitive and low-yield. Contingency recruiters are competing against other search firms and employers' own hiring efforts, and if employers decide not to fill a position or to put it on hold, they lose opportunities for income.

Therefore, contingency recruiters' time is precious. Every minute of their day is spent trying to make placements. That's why they may not call you back to let you know they received your resume. But rest assured if your background is a fit for one of their searches they will contact you, as it's money in their pocket if you get hired.

Temp and *temp-to-perm recruiters* work very much like contingency recruiters, but hire for temporary positions or positions where an employer would like to test someone out before permanently hiring him or her.

Retained recruiters search mainly for senior management positions or for positions requiring niche skill sets. Clients also use them for critical hires and confidential searches, and when they need to hire someone quickly. Like contingency recruiters, they're paid a percentage of a new hire's base salary or total compensation, plus travel expenses. Typically, they are paid one-third of their total fee up front, one-third upon reaching an agreed-upon benchmark, and the final third upon successful hire.

Corporate or *in-house recruiters* work directly for hiring employers. Companies with large HR departments sometimes have corporate recruiters on staff. They perform the same work as contingency recruiters, but exclusively for one company.

Contract recruiters function like corporate recruiters, but are hired on a short- or long-term contract basis to fill permanent, temporary, or temp-to-perm positions. Companies use contract recruiters if they have a short-term spike in hiring or if they are short-staffed because someone left. Some recruiting agencies also hire contract recruiters.

Want a Recruiter to Find You? Don't Leave Your Job

Recruiters target *passive candidates*—people who aren't looking for work. Employers prefer to hire currently employed high performers. Unfortunately, there's a stigma attached to candidates who are unemployed. For that reason, it's a mistake to quit your job just because you hate it. It's far better, in my opinion, to stick it out and seek your next job while you're still employed. Otherwise, you can add months to your job search.

Active candidates are people who are aggressively seeking new jobs. Sometimes they're unemployed; other times they sense bad times ahead for their companies and are looking to jump ship. Some employers can be more reluctant to hire overly active candidates because they fear an active candidate will take a job out of necessity, and that he'll leave once he finds more appealing work elsewhere.

Another term recruiters often use is *A-players.* These employees are the top performers in their functional area. They're difficult to acquire because they're usually compensated well. Most of them are passive candidates who come with a high price tag—and hefty recruiting fees. To entice A-players to change jobs, employers need to offer them meaningful increases in compensation, benefits, and other perks.

How to Get In Touch with Recruiters

The best way to connect with a recruiter is through LinkedIn, the number one tool recruiters use these days. Most recruiters search LinkedIn even before going to the job boards.

If you have specialized skills you may want to register with recruiting firms that cater to your industry.

What Happens When a Recruiter Looks at Your Resume

To write a resume that will hold a recruiter's attention and make her want to know more, it helps to know how recruiters read resumes. The first thing that we look for on a resume is titles. Clear titles like Director of Marketing or Sales Manager will help you stand out.

Next, we'll look to see whether you work in an industry or for a company similar to our client's.

Third, we'll scan for proven results. Therefore, always use metrics and specifics on your resume like percentages and dollar amounts. Your references should be able to confirm that you produced the results mentioned on your resume.

Recruiters will also look to see whether you've been job-hopping or have stagnated. A new job every year could indicate that you can't hold down a job, whereas staying at one job for too many years can suggest you're not able to branch out. Having a new job every four to seven years, with an increase in responsibility, scope, and territory at each one, shows you may be an easier candidate to work with.

A Recruiter Just Left Me a Message: Now What?

Say you've posted a stellar resume on LinkedIn and a recruiter's called you about a job opening at a certain company. What should you do next?

Head to Google. Recruiters will expect you to know something about the companies where they're suggesting you work. That's one reason why you should always let callers leave a message while job hunting: It gives you time to do a little homework before you call someone back. Go to companies' websites and read their press releases.

Also, determine what you want and don't want from a job. To improve your chances with recruiters, be up-front with them. Tell them exactly what you're looking for, being specific about what you want in terms of compensation, benefits, and location. At some point, a recruiter will ask you what your current compensation is and how much you're seeking from your next job. Different recruiters and HR professionals have different opinions on how you should answer this question, but I'd suggest stating a precise amount rather than giving a salary range. If you give a company a range and they do make you an offer, it will usually be at the low end of whatever range you provide them.

You can also improve your relationship with a recruiter by serving as a professional contact. Let him know about job openings at your company or potential candidates for positions he's looking to fill. In return he might be able to give you leads on jobs at other companies. However, don't disclose openings for jobs you're interested in. Some recruiters may pitch companies other candidates for those jobs, increasing your competition.

What Not to Do When Working with Recruiters

When you're dealing with a recruiter, there are a few classic mistakes you'll want to avoid. For instance, many, many job seekers confuse recruiters for their personal career counselors. They bother recruiters by calling them to check in. But recruiters are very focused on filling positions and do not need reminder calls. If you do fit the requirements for a job, then a recruiter will contact you.

The second biggest mistake people make when working with recruiters is relying too heavily on them. Keep in mind that less than 5% of open positions are filled by agency recruiters.

Make sure your resume is clear, complete, and accurate. Never lie or be misleading on your resume. Never use humor on your resume or cover letters. Employers view hiring as serious business. Humor usually backfires 90% of the time. Consider your audience: Don't just list your current and previous employers' names, but include enough information about them to give readers a good idea of what kind of companies you worked for. Avoid jargon or terminology that's only used by your company.

Precision is also important when composing your resume. List tangible and specific accomplishments. Do describe ways you solved a past employer's problems or how you will solve a future employer's. Don't write a one-size-fits-all resume but target your resume for each job you're applying to.

Don't be late to interviews, or, worse, be a no-show. If you don't show up for an interview a recruiter has gotten for you, you'll never hear from him again, now or in the future. Dress appropriately and be prepared.

Don't negotiate offers without consulting your recruiter. If you're fortunate enough to get to the offer stage, let the recruiter speak on your behalf. I've seen many candidates have offers withdrawn due to poor negotiating skills. For example, they've asked for higher base salaries than they originally requested or tell prospective employers they have other job offers and want to see who'll give them the better deal. Mistakes like those can create bad chemistry between you and your potential new employer.

Also, keep in mind that companies will take note of whatever salary figure you give them—even if it's something you just blurted out during a conversation. Don't think you can ask for more money than you originally requested, even if you did so informally. Unfortunately, I've seen many job offers withdrawn due to candidates' revising salary expectations at the last minute.

Remember, if you let the recruiter do the bidding, you don't have to be directly involved in the negotiation process. If you're waiting on another offer or receive a better offer, your recruiter can communicate that information to your potential employer and strategize on your behalf.

The Importance of Face-to-Face Networking in a Technological Society

In 2007, while I was on a business trip to Los Angeles, a client invited me to something called a wine tasting Meetup. As I soon learned, Meetup.com was a new website that used social media to help people organize interest groups in their local areas.

When guests at that event found out I was a recruiter, they asked me for advice on job hunting, resumes, and career development in addition to talking about wine, sports, and the weather. I saw how technology could be used to help people create networks, and also how integrated life, work, and job hunting had become.

At the time, there were very few Meetup networking groups in the Bay Area, so I decided to create one that would also help people network with other job seekers, potential employers, and other professionals. And, since the Napa Valley wine country is in our backyard and there are so many wine enthusiasts in the Bay Area, I decided to add a wine tasting component. I called it the Palo Alto Wine Group.

Our group provides a casual and friendly atmosphere where Bay Area professionals make new friends, meet other singles or couples, and network with business contacts through wine tasting. Events take place monthly in or near Palo Alto at upscale establishments that can accommodate over 100 attendees and serve a variety of nice wines. In my opinion, it's the best place to network in the Bay Area. Our attendees range from tech company executives to physicians, attorneys, engineers, HR professionals, salespeople, educators, venture capitalists, investors, accountants, software developers, and real estate professionals.

Our group has helped many people find jobs. One of my favorite stories is the time a member bumped into the woman who had interviewed him six months earlier at one of our events. He had never heard back from her and had always wondered what happened to the job. The woman told him that the position had been put on hold because the firm postponed its budget, but that there was now enough funding in place to reopen the job requisition. She invited him to re-interview for the position and he got the job.

Another time, a colleague of mine was looking for a specific position with a company he thought he'd be a perfect fit for. He brought it up in conversation with an executive while they were sharing a blind tasting of 2010 Napa Cabernets. She offered to forward his resume to a key executive she knew at the firm, and my colleague was flown in the following week for an interview.

Another example was a woman who had just moved from Washington, DC to the Bay Area and had joined Meetup to network and make friends. Her goal at one of our events was to meet people from three specific firms she had targeted for her job search. By mingling and chatting, by the end of the night she had not only met employees of her target firms, but had also learned inside information about the firms' hiring processes and had gotten a list of follow-up contacts.

The Palo Alto Wine Group started off with just a few members who were friends who needed help with their resumes. Since then it has expanded to over 4,000 members with subgroups for everyone, including singles, couples, wine connoisseurs, people just learning about wine, people who want to network, and those who just want to have fun while enjoying a glass of wine. It's a very friendly group and you will always see familiar faces as well as new people. I estimate each event has about 33% regulars, 33% first timers, and 33% occasional attendees. If you live in the Palo Alto area, I encourage you to attend. I would be happy to critique your resume if you bring it with you.

CHAPTER SEVEN

Your Career Adventure

A Framework for Planning Your Career

As we've seen, the workplace has changed dramatically over the past few decades. People are living much longer, meaning they must also work longer and keep a careful eye on their finances to ensure they'll have enough to live on. The workforce has become incredibly diverse in terms of gender, race, nationality, generation, and family patterns. New technologies are invented all the time, creating and destroying job categories, and so workers have to continually update their skills to remain employable. And not only companies but individuals face competition from abroad.

At the same time, workers have more options than ever before. They may choose to work for large corporations, medium-sized firms, or small businesses; work in the public, private, or nonprofit sectors; start their own businesses or operate franchises; freelance; or do some combination of the above. They now have greater freedom to choose the working arrangements that best suit their temperaments, skill sets, interests, and values, and change their employers or working conditions to suit different phases of their lives. As a result, their career and life paths resemble mazes more than they do ladders (see Figure 7.1).

Are You Ready?

Which do you spend more time planning—your career or your next vacation? If you're like most people, the answer's the latter. Americans spend an average of five hours planning a vacation, five hours researching a home loan, eight hours pre-

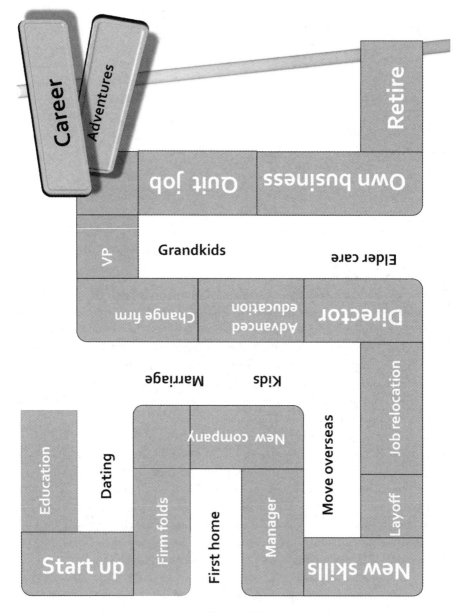

Figure 7.1

paring to buy a car, and 10 hours planning a major home improvement project.[1] Even busy working adults with children dedicate an average of 2.5 hours a day to leisure and sports.[2]

But college seniors—the very people you'd think would be most invested in career planning—spend less time preparing for their careers than they do partying or surfing the Internet. Seventy-two percent of college seniors spend less than two hours a week career planning, and 15% spend no time at all. And only about 40% of Americans formally plan their careers.[3]

In particular, people aren't prepared for extreme longevity. For our last book, *Women Lead*, we interviewed over 200 female leaders, asking them about their careers and secrets to success. One of the questions we asked these women was how the prospect of living to 100 changed how they thought about their careers. It was clear that many of them had never considered the implications of living that long. When they gave the question more thought, many noted that they might need to work until 80 to have enough money to live on for another 20 years. They expressed concern about staying healthy, balanced, educated, and technically proficient enough to remain employed for 50 or 60 years.

Career planning doesn't have to be arduous, and you don't have to map your career down to the last detail. In fact, given how protean careers are these days, and how quickly life circumstances can change, it doesn't make sense to plan too meticulously. But constructing a single-page framework for your career can be very helpful. It can give you an idea of what you value, where and for whom you want to work, and what kind of money, time, and training you'll need to reach your goals. And it will get you started thinking about the future—even about what's going to happen to you decades from now—reducing the chances that you'll approach old age unprepared.

Create a Personal Plan for Your Life

The Ford Motor Company recently ran a series of commercials asking, "Who's healthier, you or your car?" Most people interviewed in the ads responded that their car was healthier than they were because they took their car in for regular inspections and tune-ups, but didn't get yearly checkups or follow any kind of plan to improve their health. These ads make the point that we often put more thought into the maintenance of our disposable assets than the care of our own bodies.

And the same's often true of our careers, values, and life goals. That's why it can be helpful to sit down for an hour or two and make a plan, one that incorporates such areas of your life as work, finances, education, social and family life, and hobbies and leisure. We've created a simple framework to serve as a starting point. To use it, create a chart that looks like the one in Figure 7.2.

Then, fill in the blanks with what you plan or planned to be doing in each area of your life in each decade. Alter the chart categories as you see fit. If it makes

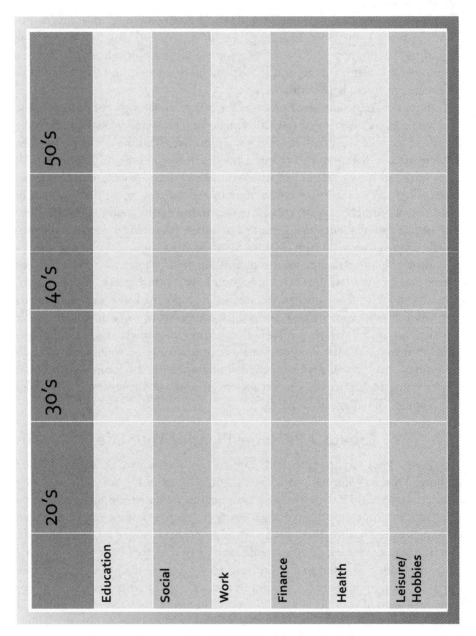

Figure 7.2, part 1

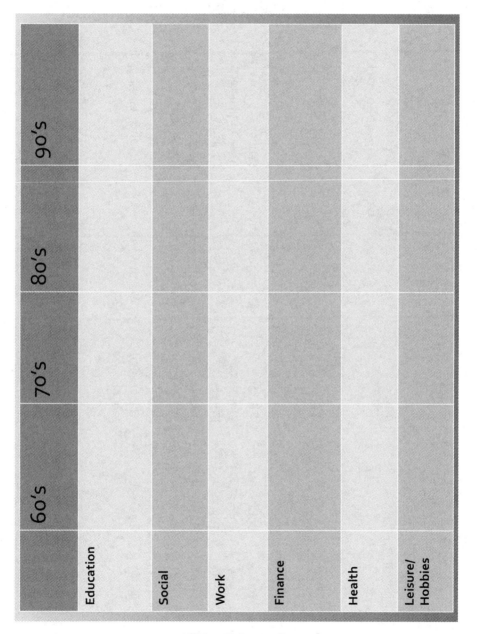

Figure 7.2, part 2

	20's	30's	40's	50's
Education	BA	MA	Learn more communications skills	Learn more communications skills
Social	Single, bought house	Married, baby, sold 1st house, bought 2nd one	Live abroad for a year	Empty nest
Work	Journalism, freelance on the side	PR for university, freelance	Communications	Senior communications position
Finance	Mortgage, invest and save	Mortgage, college fund for baby	Invest, save more for retirement	Invest, save more for retirement
Health	Basketball	Basketball, weights, cycling	Weights, cycling, diet	Weights, cycling, diet
Leisure/ Hobbies	Pottery, photography, travel	Cooking, photography, travel	Cooking, photography, travel	More international travel

Figure 7.3, part 1

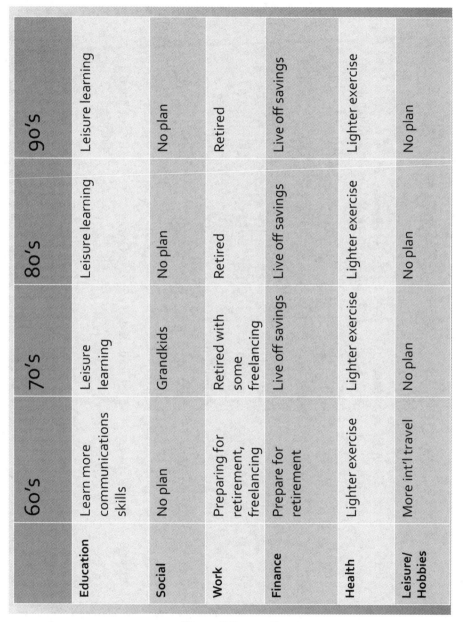

	60's	70's	80's	90's
Education	Learn more communications skills	Leisure learning	Leisure learning	Leisure learning
Social	No plan	Grandkids	No plan	No plan
Work	Preparing for retirement, freelancing	Retired with some freelancing	Retired	Retired
Finance	Prepare for retirement	Live off savings	Live off savings	Live off savings
Health	Lighter exercise	Lighter exercise	Lighter exercise	Lighter exercise
Leisure/ Hobbies	More int'l travel	No plan	No plan	No plan

Figure 7.3, part 2

	20's	30's	40's	50's
Education	BA + MBA	PhD + Tech skills	Postdoc + Tech skills	Tech skill refresh
Social	Dating, 1st home	Married, friends	Married, 2nd home, friends	Friends + Travel
Work	Jobs, 2 layoffs, relocation	Lateral moves, career definition	Director, VP	Layoff/self employed
Finance	Save money	Invest money	Grow money	Refine portfolio
Health	Diet + Fitness	Diet + Fitness	Refine Diet + Fitness	Strength and Nutrition
Leisure/ Hobbies	Travel, writing, teaching	Travel, writing, teaching, speaking	Travel, writing, speaking	Hobby = Career

Figure 7.4, part 1

	60's	70's	80's	90's
Education	Biz/Tech skills	Ad hoc learning	Ad hoc learning	Ad hoc learning
Social	Friends and family care	Friends and family care	Friends and family care	Friends and family care
Work	Self-employed	Self-employed	Part-time work	Active
Finance	Re-evaluate portfolio	Assess savings	Live off savings	Live off savings
Health	Diet, stretching	Diet, balance	Diet, walking	Diet, walking
Leisure/ Hobbies	Travel	Travel	Travel	Travel

Figure 7.4, part 2

	20's	30's	40's	50's
Education	BA	MBA, tech certification	Business classes	Tech tutorials
Social	Dating	Married, 1st home, friends	Married, 2nd home, friends	Friends
Work	Corporate work, relocation	Layoff, start business	Grow business	Expand business
Finance	Save, invest money	Save, invest money	Save, invest in business	Save, invest in business
Health	Diet, weights	Diet, weights	Refine diet, adjust fitness	Refine diet, adjust fitness
Leisure/ Hobbies	Vacation, flying	Travel, wine tasting, biking, hiking	Biking, wine group	Biking, wine group, guitar

Figure 7.5, part 1

	60's	70's	80's	90's
Education	Ad hoc learning	Ad hoc learning	Ad hoc learning	Ad hoc learning
Social	Friends	Friends	Friends	Friends
Work	Expand business	Enjoy business	Part-time business	Active in business
Finance	Re-evaluate portfolio	Assess savings	Live off savings	Live off savings
Health	Adjust diet and fitness	Adjust diet and fitness	Adjust diet and fitness	Adjust diet and fitness
Leisure/ Hobbies	Vacation, wine group	Vacation, wine group	Vacation, wine group	Vacation, wine group

Figure 7.5, part 2

	20's	30's	40's	50's
Education	Degree Certification Job training	Work training MBA Leadership	Tech classes Finance classes Programming	Business classes PhD Master's degree
Social/Family	Dating Marriage Partners	1st child 1st home Friends	2nd child Larger home Family	Vacation home Work friends Kids' activities
Work	First job 1st layoff Join Startup	New job Manager Relocation	Change firms Director Lateral job move	Overseas rotation Vice President Layoff
Finance	Pay off debt Rent Start saving	Mortgage 401k Mutual funds	Invest stock College fund Buy rental property	Sell 1st home Bonds Child's wedding
Health	Running Weight control Rugby	Gym Nutrition Skiing	Triathlon Beauty routine Tennis	Jogging Genetic test Biking
Leisure/Hobbies	Flight school Camping Blogging	Writing books Eco-travel Junior League	Volunteering Cooking Wine tasting	RV Trips Mahjong Ballroom dancing

Figure 7.6, part 1

	60's	70's	80's	90's
Education	Finance talks Retirement talks Gerontology ed.	Health talks Tech classes Adult ed.	Travel talks Community ed. World event talks	Religion talks Leisure learning Meditation class
Social/Family	Remarry Neighborhood Second home	Build home Alumni Grandkids	Church events Great-grandkids Family reunions	Senior center Family visits Senior socials
Work	Consulting Start business Expand business	Part-time work Home office Freelance	Retirement Non-profit Eldercare	Sell firm Volunteer Leave biz. to kids
Finance	Trust funds Grandkids' tuition Pay off homes	Pension Investments Life-care home	IRA Sell assets Consolidate finances	Review will Social Security Live on savings
Health	Hiking Vitamins Swimming	Strength train Supplements Yoga	Balance train Diet assessment Pilates	Walking Organic diet Tai Chi
Leisure/Hobbies	Politics Global travel Interior design	Babysitting Pet sitting Music	Golf Bird watching Bridge	Woodwork Painting Gardening

Figure 7.6, part 2

more sense for you to plan in five-year increments than decades, or even to plan a single year quarter-by-quarter or month-by-month, go ahead and do so. You may also want to add rows for other areas of your life: If you've got a major life goal in mind, for example, like traveling to every continent, writing a novel, or hiking the Appalachian Trail, make a row for it.

For decades you've already lived through, fill in both what your plan was and what actually happened during those years. If you didn't have a plan, put "no plan." It may be useful to reflect on what impact planning, or the lack thereof, had on your life today.

Fill out the framework in as much or as little detail as you find appropriate. If you're a goal-oriented person who likes making and executing specific plans, you'll probably add more detail than an opportunity-oriented person who antici-pates that unforeseen circumstances will drive her career. But both spontaneous and methodical types can benefit from making a plan, even if it's a loose one, and from thinking ahead.

There are no right or wrong answers here. If you have no plan for a certain area of your life at a certain decade, then be honest and put down "no plan." Then go back and give these areas more thought. You may determine that you do, in fact, need to make a plan for them.

Society treats work, family and social life, and leisure time as separate spheres, but, in practice, they're deeply intertwined. Your family structure often helps de-termine where you work and who you work for—you may not want to relocate when your children are small, for example, but be more open to moving once they're older—which, in turn, affects how much free time you have for hobbies and exercise. Your desire to live abroad for a while may mean you take a job at a large corporation with a branch in Italy rather than a comparable position with a smaller firm.

This chart is meant to be a flexible tool that prompts you to reflect on your life as a system of interconnecting realms. It's a way to help you see the con-nections between life events: How have your finances impacted your social and family choices? How do your life goals affect the choices you make about work, finances, and how you spend your time? Ultimately, it's meant to get you thinking about how to reach an equilibrium and attain your personal definition of success.

Sample Frameworks

We've provided some sample frameworks to give you an idea of how other people filled them out. Figure 7.3 was completed by a Millennial who pursued a career in journalism in his 20s. After realizing that the newspaper industry was in decline, he acquired skills in website development and graphic design and entered the communications field. He is now pursuing a master's degree in technology and communications as preparation for a director-level position.

Figure 7.4 is a framework filled out by a female Baby Boomer who climbed the corporate ladder from manager to director to vice president. After being unexpectedly laid off in her 40s, she found new opportunities in consulting, and now focuses on traveling, leading a healthy lifestyle, and having fun.

Figure 7.5 is a framework completed by a Generation Xer who, in his 20s, set a goal of owning a business by age 40. To do so, he took a corporate job in a more promising location than the region he grew up in, spending nights and weekends working on his business plan. In his 30s, an unexpected layoff presented him with the opportunity to start his company earlier than he expected. Today he owns three firms, is married, and lives in his dream location.

Finally, Figure 7.6 is an aggregate framework summarizing the responses of many different people. It hints at the wide variety of plans, goals, and strategies people make at various stages in their lives, and will likely spark some ideas.

Prompt Questions

As a further aid to filling out the framework, here are some questions to jog your memory and get you thinking:

Work:

- Do you want to work? For how long?

- What kind, or kinds, of work will keep you employed and engaged for 50 years?

- What's most important to you in a job: Salary? Stability? Benefits? Opportunities for advancement? Intellectual stimulation? Creativity? Values such as community service or helping the environment?

- What are your strengths and weaknesses as a worker?

- What kind of setting do you want to work in: A large corporation? A small business? Your own home? Would you rather be your own boss or work for someone else?

- What are your work goals?

- What kinds of skills, education, and experience will you need to meet these goals? To stay employable?

Finances

- What kind of financial obligations do you anticipate having at each stage of your life? A mortgage? Paying off college loans? Sending a dependent to college? Healthcare costs for you or your relatives? Educational or training costs for yourself? Enough money for vacations and leisure?

- How much money will you need to meet these obligations over a year? Over a lifetime? How will you earn enough?

- Say you'll live to 100—something that's certainly not out of the question these days. How will you make enough to support yourself until then?

- When do you plan to retire? What kind of lifestyle would you find acceptable in retirement? How much money would you need to sustain this lifestyle?

- How do you plan to earn, save, or invest your money?

Health

- How will you prepare yourself to stay healthy into old age? Are there lifestyle changes you'll need to make: Improving your diet? Giving up smoking? Drinking less? Exercising more?

- How will you stay active at each phase of your life?

- What are your fitness goals?

Education

- What knowledge or skills will you need at each stage of your career?

- How will you acquire knowledge and skills? Degree programs? Certificate programs? One-time classes or seminars? Training provided by your employer? Online classes or tutorials? Reading books, journals, or web articles? Joining professional organizations? Attending conferences?

- How much money and time will it take to acquire these skills?

Social/Family

- What do you want your social or family life to look like in each decade of your life? Do you plan on dating, getting married or finding a partner, having or adopting children, or taking care of grandchildren? Will you have eldercare responsibilities?

- How will your family and social obligations affect your career?

- How will you make friends and community connections: Volunteering? Church? Meetup groups? Other groups centered around your hobbies or interests?

- Where do you plan to live? Do you want to buy a house or rent? In what part of the country or world? Are you open to relocating for work or other reasons? Will you change your living arrangements in retirement?

Leisure

- What are your interests, passions, and hobbies? How much money and time will you need to engage in them?

- Are there new interests you want to pursue later on in life?

- Would you want your hobby to become or contribute to your work?

Other

- Are there other aspects of your life or life goals that don't fit in any of these categories?

Follow-Up

Once you've completed the chart, think about what you've learned from the process of filling it out. You may want to jot your thoughts down for further reflection. In particular, consider:

- *Gaps.* Are there areas where you have no plan? (If so, you're not alone; many of us haven't given much thought to what we'll do decades into the future.) If so, do you *need* a plan yet for these areas? (Not knowing what you'll do for fun in your 80s may not be as important as being unsure what your finances will look like in five years.) Are there areas where you need more information to be able to plan?

- *Areas that need more specifics.* Likewise, are there are any areas where you have a loose plan but would like a more detailed one? For example, do you need to give some more thought to which certifications you'll need for your job in five years' time? Do you need to determine exactly how much it will cost to retire and preserve your current standard of living?

- *Patterns.* Are there any common threads running through your life or career? Are you more likely to meet your goals when you make concrete plans or when you take risks? When were you most satisfied with your work and home life, and why? When were you least satisfied, and why? What values have guided your life and career? What happened when you deviated from those values?

- *Pivot points.* Consider times when you made a career or lifestyle change. What prompted those changes? Were you happy with the decisions you made? If you could go back to those points in time, what would you do differently?

- *Goals.* What steps do you need to take reach your goals? What can you be doing today that can help you get closer to a distant goal? For example, one woman who filled out this framework set a goal of working in China in the next 10 to 15 years. She realized that to do so, she'd need to learn some Mandarin; research living and working abroad, including job opportunities and legal requirements; find a job with a multinational company with branches in China; gain the types of experiences within that company that would enable her to be sent overseas; and determine what to do with her house.

Notes

1. Zillow, "Americans Spend More Time Researching Car Purchase than Their Home Loan, According to Recent Zillow.com® Survey," news release, April 3, 2008, http://www.reuters.com/article/2008/04/03/idUS126258+03-Apr-2008+PRN20080403.
2. US Bureau of Labor Statistics, "Charts from the American Time Use Survey," last modified July 10, 2013, http://www.bls.gov/tus/charts/.
3. Thomas J. Denham, "I Don't Know What I Want, But This Ain't Doing It," *About.com*, accessed August 14, 2013, http://jobsearch.about.com/od/careeradvice/a/transition.htm.

A Parting Word

The new world of do-it-yourself careers brings both promise and peril. Many people long for the old days when they could expect to work for the same company, or at least in the same industry, for an extended amount of time. And, frankly, we don't blame them. Long jobs gave workers a sense of security, stability, community, and identity along with the tangible advantages of a salary, benefits, and a retirement plan they could count on. And having to train for a new job or career, particularly when you had anticipated staying in your old one, can be scary and a drain on your time, energy, and finances.

But we encourage you to also see the positive side of the new career landscape. For instance, you don't have to feel locked into the same career path you chose when you were in your twenties. Though your finances and family situation will always have a great deal to do with where you work and for whom, you still have considerable freedom to change your employer and working conditions as your life circumstances change. Thanks to the Internet, you have the ability to find or create working arrangements that suit you, you're better able to network, and you're more informed about employers, industries, and skill requirements. You can even train for little to no cost online. And learning new skills and knowledge, while challenging, is also invigorating.

Those of you who are more fond of novelty and taking risks likely welcome the prospect of reinventing your career every decade or so. But embracing an entrepreneurial mindset towards your career is helpful even if you prefer stability:

Staying current with skill requirements and keeping abreast of new technologies can help you remain with the same employer or in the same industry if that's your goal.

So, while today's fast-paced, technology-driven career landscape can seem intimidating, it's also ripe with opportunities to customize the career that's right for you. We hope the advice we've provided in this book will help you to navigate this landscape and remain employed for life.

Summary of Key Points

- *Societal shifts have changed work forever.* Family patterns are dramatically different than they were a few decades ago. More women are in the workforce and more men are interested in work-life balance. Employers who want to retain the best talent will need to innovate new career development structures that make sense for workers with family obligations. The US workforce has also become much more diverse in terms of ethnicity, country of origin, and generation, meaning employees will need to develop cultural competence, be open to diverse viewpoints, and hone the social skills that will help them build teams with diverse colleagues.

- *Extended longevity has increased the need for career planning.* To stay employable for a career that could last 50 years, workers need to continually refresh their skills and keep abreast of trends in their industries. They must also plan their finances with care to ensure they have enough savings to keep them afloat through lengthy retirements.

- *Keeping up with technology is critical.* Technology both creates and destroys jobs, and innovations continually disrupt entire industries. Today's employees need to stay current with technologies that are potential game-changers for their fields, and learn to use the most important technological tools in their industries.

- *The face of corporate career development is changing.* According to HR professionals, companies offer fewer structured career tracks and perform less training than they once did. But companies are now more open to nontraditional career tracks that allow for lateral moves and career breaks. They are also developing non-management career tracks for specialists and using social media for learning and development. Companies should strive to make their development processes transparent, HR experts say, and do more to integrate managers into career development.

- *HR professionals recommend the following best practices for individual career development:* taking initiative and not letting your career just happen; using all the resources your firm has to offer; sharing your career plan with your superiors; and expanding your network.

- *Recruiters suggest the following best practices for individual career development:* marketing yourself so you stand out against a sea of other candidates; having an impeccable resume that lists concrete accomplishments; and networking, especially by using LinkedIn.

- *To work successfully with recruiters,* know what you want in terms of salary, benefits, and responsibility; learn about the companies they suggest you work for; be professional when applying for jobs; and allow them to negotiate on your behalf. Know that recruiters' time is precious and trust that they will get back to you if they've found a job opening you fit. When recruiters read resumes, they look for clear titles, quantifiable results, and whether you've held jobs for too brief or too long a time.

- *To thrive in a VUCA job market, workers will need planning, foresight, and constant reskilling.* Like the business world itself, the world of careers has become *v*olatile, *u*ncertain, *c*omplex, and *a*mbiguous. To stay employable workers will need to stay agile, plan well, welcome change, research trends, and continually refresh their skills and knowledge.

- *Today is the right time to build a career that fulfills all aspects of your life.* Workers today have more choices than ever before: They can freelance, start companies, own franchises, take flexible working arrangements, work for large corporations or small or medium-sized businesses, or take jobs in the public or nonprofit sectors. All these options give employees great freedom to design careers that bring their work, family, social, financial, physical, and intellectual lives into balance. Through staying actively engaged in career planning, they can increase their chances of remaining happily employed for life.

REFERENCES

AARP. *Baby Boomers Envision Retirement II: Survey of Baby Boomers' Expectations for Retirement.* Washington, DC: AARP, 2004. http://assets.aarp.org/rgcenter/econ/boomers_envision.pdf.

ACUA. "Education & Careers." Accessed August 5, 2013. http://www.acuaonline.org/education-careers.

Adler, Roy D. "Profit, Thy Name Is . . . Woman?" *Pacific Standard*, February 27, 2009. http://www.psmag.com/business-economics/profit-thy-name-is-woman-3920/.

Aguilar, Lauren. "The Myth of the Ideal Worker: New Workforce, Outdated Workplace." *Gender News* (blog). The Clayman Institute for Gender Research, April 16, 2012. http://gender.stanford.edu/news/2012/myth-ideal-worker-new-workforce-outdated-workplace.

American Express. *The American Express OPEN State of Women-Owned Businesses Report.* New York: American Express, 2011. http://media.nucleus.naprojects.com/pdf/WomanReport_FINAL.pdf.

Associated Press. "Can Smart Machines Take Your Job? Middle Class Jobs Increasingly Being Replaced by Technology." *New York Daily News*, January 24, 2013. http://www.nydailynews.com/news/national/smart-machines-job-article-1.1246522.

———. "More Data and the Cloud Help Replace Humans—and Their Salaries—on the Job," *Omaha World Herald*, January 24, 2013. http://www.omaha.com/article/20130124/MONEY/701249997/1707.

Bailyn, Lotte. "Redesigning Work for Gender Equity and Work-Personal Life Integration." *Community, Work & Family* 14 (2011), 102.

Beaman, Karen V. *2011–2012 Going Global Report: HCM Trends in Globalization.* San Francisco: Jeitosa Group International, 2011. http://www.jeitosa.com/wp-content/uploads/2011/12/Going-Global-Report-HCM-Trends-in-Globalization-FINAL-IHRIMWire-DEC-2011-1-PGV.pdf.

Benko, Cathleen and Anne Weisberg. *Mass Career Customization: Aligning the Workplace with Today's Nontraditional Workforce.* Cambridge, MA: Harvard Business School, 2007.

Berry, Peter, Shayne Nealon, and Kim Pluess. *Female Leadership in Australia.* Northbridge, Australia: 2008. http://www.peterberry.com.au/files//white_papers/pbc_white_paper_-_female_leadership_in_australia_berry_nealon__pluess.pdf. Men scored higher than women on control-and-command leadership and bottom-line thinking.

Bersin, Josh. "A New Organizational Learning Model: Learning On-Demand." *Bersin by Deloitte* (blog), October 1, 2007. http://joshbersin.com/2007/10/01/a-new-organizational-learning-model-learning-on-demand/.

Bianchi, Suzanne M. "Changing Families, Changing Workplaces." *The Future of Children* 21, no. 2 (2011): 15–36.

Binns, Corey. "Twendy-One Nursebot Says Sit Up and Eat Your Jell-O." *Popular Science*, July 8, 2009. http://www.popsci.com/scitech/article/2009-06/machines-heal.

Bolick, Kate. "Single People Deserve Work-Life Balance, Too." *The Atlantic*, June 28, 2012. http://www.theatlantic.com/business/archive/2012/06/single-people-deserve-work-life-balance-too/259071/.

Bollier, David. *The Future of Work: What It Means for Individuals, Businesses, Markets and Governments*. Washington, DC: The Aspen Institute, 2011. http://www.aspeninstitute.org/sites/default/files/content/docs/pubs/The_Future_of_Work.pdf.

Bosco, Susan M. and Candy A. Bianco. "Influence of Maternal Work Patterns and Socioeconomic Status on Gen Y Lifestyle Choice." *Journal of Career Development* 32, no. 2 (2005): 165-82.

Boston.com and Monster.com. "10 Jobs in Decline through 2020." Accessed December 5, 2012. http://www.boston.com/jobs/galleries/10_jobs_in_decline/.

Bowers, Elaine. "Dads Dive Into the Stay-at-Home Role." *ParentMap*, February 3, 2009. http://www.parentmap.com/article/dads-dive-into-the-stay-at-home-role.

Brown, David A. H., Debra L. Brown, and Vanessa Anastasopoulos. *Women on Boards: Not Just the Right Thing . . . But the "Bright" Thing*. Ottawa: The Conference Board of Canada, 2002. http://www.europeanpwn.net/files/women_on_boards_canada.pdf.

Bryzek, Janusz. "Emergences of a $Trillion MEMS Sensor Market." Fairchild Semiconductor. Presentation slides. http://www.sensorscon.org/English/Archives/201203/Presentations/Janusz_Bryzek_SensorsCon2012.pdf.

Bugin, Jacques, Michael Chui, and James Manyika. "Clouds, Big Data, and Smart Assets: Ten Tech-Enabled Business Trends to Watch." *McKinsey Quarterly*, August 2010. https://www.mckinseyquarterly.com/Clouds_big_data_and_smart_assets_Ten_tech-enabled_business_trends_to_watch_2647.

Business and Professional Women's Foundation. *From Gen Y Women to Employers: What They Want in the Workplace and Why It Matters for Business*. Business and Professional Women's Foundation, 2011. http://www.bpwfoundation.org/documents/uploads/YC_SummaryReport_Final_Web.pdf.

Cabrera, Elizabeth F. "Opting Out and Opting In: Understanding the Complexities of Women's Career Transitions." *Career Development International* 12, no. 3 (2007): 218–37. http://e-archivo.uc3m.es/bitstream/10016/11270/1/opting_cabrera_CDI_2007_ps.pdf.

Cahill, Kevin H., Michael D. Giandrea, and Joseph F. Quinn. "Reentering the Labor Force after Retirement." *Monthly Labor Review*, June 2011, 34–42.

Callahan, Rebecca. "Blended Workforce: The New Norm." *Talent Management*, September 9, 2011. http://talentmgt.com/articles/view/blended-workforce-the-new-norm/print:1.

Carter, Joanne. "Top 10 iPad and iPhone Wedding Photography Apps." *The App Whisperer*, May 29, 2011. http://theappwhisperer.com/2011/05/29/top-10-ipad-and-iphone-wedding-photography-apps/.

Casey, Judi, and Barbara Denton. "Effective Workplace Series. Work-Family Information on: Generation X/Generation Y." *Sloan Work and Family Research Network*, March 2008. https://workfamily.sas.upenn.edu/sites/workfamily.sas.upenn.edu/files/imported/pdfs/EWS_GenXandY.pdf.

Center for Women's Business Research. *The Economic Impact of Women-Owned Businesses in the United States*. McLean, VA: Center for Women's Business Research, 2009. http://www.womensbusinessresearchcenter.org/Data/research/economicimpactstud/econimpactreport-final.pdf.

Chua, Jasmin Malik. "LED-Equipped Solar Timbuk2 Bag Creates a FLAP at PopTech." *Ecouterre*, October 23, 2009. http://www.ecouterre.com/led-equipped-solar-timbuk2-bag-creates-a-flap-at-poptech/.

Cisco. *The Future of Work: Information Access Expectations, Demand, and Behavior of the World's Next-Generation Workforce.* San Jose, CA: Cisco, 2011. Presentation slides. http://www.cisco.com/en/US/solutions/ns341/ns525/ns537/ns705/ns1120/cisco_connected_world_technology_report_chapter2_press_deck.pdf.

―――. *Transitioning to Workforce 2020.* San Jose: Cisco, 2011. http://www.cisco.com/web/learning/employer_resources/pdfs/Workforce_2020_White_Paper.pdf.

CNNMoney. "Global 500. Full List. 2012." July 23, 2012. http://money.cnn.com/magazines/fortune/global500/2012/full_list/.

―――. "Index to the Fortune Global 500." August 2, 1999. http://money.cnn.com/magazines/fortune/fortune_archive/1999/08/02/263627/index.htm.

Collamer, Nancy. "5 Tips for Getting a Government Job." *Forbes,* November 14, 2012. http://www.forbes.com/sites/nextavenue/2012/11/14/5-tips-for-getting-a-government-job/.

College Online. "Are Librarians Totally Obsolete?" Accessed August 3, 2013. http://www.collegeonline.org/library/adult-continued-education/librarians-needed.html.

Collins, Patrick, and Adriano Autino. "What the Growth of a Space Tourism Industry Could Contribute to Employment, Economic Growth, Environmental Protection, Education, Culture and World Peace." *Space Future,* May 25, 2008. http://www.spacefuture.com/archive/what_the_growth_of_a_space_tourism_industry_could_contribute_to_employment_economic_growth_environmental_protection_education_culture_and_world_peace.shtml.

Conner, Marcia. "Time to Build Your Big-Data Muscles." *Fast Company,* July 17, 2012. http://www.fastcompany.com/1842928/time-build-your-big-data-muscles.

Cox, Lauren. "We Will Live Longer in 2050, Study Predicts." *ABC News,* December 14, 2009. http://abcnews.go.com/Health/ActiveAging/humans-live-longer-2050-scientists-predict/story?id=9330511#.UaKEukDCaSo.

Crosman, Penny, and Mary Wisniewski. "Top 10 Mobile Banking Apps." *American Banker,* February 25, 2013. http://www.americanbanker.com/gallery/top-ten-mobile-banking-apps-1057018-1.html.

Davidson, Paul. "Freelance Workers Reshape Companies and Jobs." *USA Today,* October 13, 2010. http://usatoday30.usatoday.com/money/economy/employment/2010-10-13-1Acontractworkers13_CV_N.htm; blended.

DeBois, Monica. "Showrooming: The New Wave of Retail Shopping." *The Inside Scoop* (blog). *Media Works,* March 15, 2013. http://mediaworksltd.wordpress.com/2013/03/15/showrooming-the-new-wave-of-retail-shopping.

Deloitte. *The 2011 Shift Index: Measuring the Forces of Long-Term Change.* New York: Deloitte, 2011. http://www.deloitte.com/assets/dcom-unitedstates/local%20assets/documents/us_tmt_2011shiftindex_111011.pdf.

―――. *Human Capital Trends 2012: Leap Ahead.* New York: Deloitte, 2012. http://www.deloitte.com/assets/Dcom-UnitedStates/Local%20Assets/Documents/us_cons_hctrends12_022312.pdf.

Denham, Thomas J. "I Don't Know What I Want, But This Ain't Doing It." *About.com.* Accessed August 14, 2013. http://jobsearch.about.com/od/careeradvice/a/transition.htm.

Desvaux, Georges, Sandrine Devillard-Hoellinger, and Pascal Baumgarten. *Women Matter: Gender Diversity, a Corporate Performance Driver.* Washington, DC: McKinsey 2007. http://www.europeanpwn.net/files/mckinsey_2007_gender_matters.pdf.

Dewhurst, Martin, Suzanne Heywood, and Jon Harris, "The Global Company's Challenge." *McKinsey Quarterly,* June 2012. https://www.mckinseyquarterly.com/The_global_companys_challenge_2979.

Diaz, Jesus. "Layar: First Mobile Augmented Reality Browser Is Your Real Life HUD." *Gizmodo*, June 16, 2009. http://gizmodo.com/5292748/layar-first-mobile-augmented-reality-browser-is-your-real-life-hud.

DL-ERC. "The Autonomous Vehicle Technology." Accessed August 3, 2013. http://www.dl-erc.org/component/content/article/1-electronic-research-collection-category/4-the-autonomous-vehicle-technology.

Dobbs, Jason, with Patrick Healey, Katherine Kane, Daniel Mak, and Tay K. McNamara. *The Multi-Generational Workplace*. Chestnut Hill, MA: The Sloan Center on Aging & Work at Boston College, 2007. http://www.bc.edu/content/dam/files/research_sites/agingandwork/pdf/publications/FS09_MultiGenWorkplace.pdf.

Dorrier, Jason. "Moshe Vardi: Robots Could Put Humans Out of Work By 2045." *Singularity Hub*, May 15, 2013. http://singularityhub.com/2013/05/15/moshe-vardi-robots-could-put-humans-out-of-work-by-2045/.

Duhigg, Charles. "How Companies Learn Your Secrets." *New York Times*, February 16, 2012, http://www.nytimes.com/2012/02/19/magazine/shopping-habits.html?pagewanted=all&_r=0.

The Economist. "The Mighty Middle." October 20, 2012. http://www.economist.com/news/business/21564893-medium-sized-firms-are-unsung-heroes-america%E2%80%99s-economy.

———. "The Rich World's Quiet Revolution: Women Are Gradually Taking Over the Workplace." December 30, 2009. http://www.economist.com/node/15174489.

Edmonds, Rick, Emily Guskin, Tom Rosenstiel, and Amy Mitchell. "Newspapers: By the Numbers." *The State of the News Media 2012*. Accessed August 6, 2013. http://stateofthemedia.org/2012/newspapers-building-digital-revenues-proves-painfully-slow/newspapers-by-the-numbers/.

Elance. "Freelance Talent Report." June 2011. https://www.elance.com/q/freelance-talent-report-2011.

———. "Global Small Business Survey Uncovers Online Workforce Is the New Face of Economic Recovery." News release. June 13, 2012. https://www.elance.com/q/node/1352.

Elgin, Jeff. "Top 10 Reasons to Buy a Franchise." *Entrepreneur*, December 27, 2007. http://www.entrepreneur.com/article/188452.

Engardio, Pete, with Michael Arndt and Dean Foust. "The Future of Outsourcing." *Businessweek*, January 29, 2006. http://www.businessweek.com/stories/2006-01-29/the-future-of-outsourcing.

Erickson, Tamara. "Don't Treat Them Like Baby Boomers."*Businessweek*, August 13, 2008. http://www.businessweek.com/stories/2008-08-13/dont-treat-them-like-baby-boomers.

Ernst, Kurt. "BMW Works to Perfect the Virtual Test Drive." *MotorAuthority*, April 24, 2012. http://www.motorauthority.com/news/1075654_bmw-works-to-perfect-the-virtual-test-drive.

Estrela, Julia. "Underwater Hotels in the Florida Keys." *eHow*. Accessed August 5, 2013. http://www.ehow.com/list_6834841_underwater-hotels-florida-keys.html.

Ewing Marion Kauffman Foundation, "An Entrepreneurial Generation of 18- to 34-Year-Olds Wants to Start Companies When Economy Rebounds, According to New Poll." News release. November 10, 2011. http://www.kauffman.org/newsroom/millennials-want-to-start-companies-when-economy-rebounds-poll-says.aspx.

Families and Work Institute. *Tips for Managers. Generation & Gender in the Workforce*. New York: Families and Work Institute, 2009. http://familiesandwork.org/site/research/reports/GG-managertips.pdf.

Fiscal Policy Institute. *Immigrant Small Business Owners: A Significant and Growing Part of the Economy*. New York: Fiscal Policy Institute, 2012. http://fiscalpolicy.org/immigrant-small-business-owners-a-significant-and-growing-part-of-the-economy.

Fortune. "100 Best Companies to Work For." February 4, 2013. http://money.cnn.com/magazines/fortune/best-companies/2013/snapshots/3.html?iid=bc_sp_list.

Fraone, Jennifer Sabatini, Danielle Hartmann, and Kristin McNally. *The Multi-Generational Workforce: Management Implications and Strategies for Collaboration.* Chestnut Hill, MA: Boston College Center for Work & Family, 2007. http://www.bc.edu/content/dam/files/centers/cwf/research/publications/pdf/MultiGen_EBS.pdf.

Freedman, Marc. *Encore: Finding Work That Matters in the Second Half of Life.* New York: PublicAffairs, 2008. Kindle edition.

Fried, Ina. "Apple's Scott Forstall on How 'Project Purple' Became the iPhone." *All Things D*, August 3, 2012. http://allthingsd.com/20120803/apples-scott-forstall-on-how-project-purple-turned-into-the-iphone/.

Friedman, Thomas L. *The World Is Flat: A Brief History of the Twenty-First Century,* 2nd ed. New York: Farrar, Straus and Giroux, 2006.

Galinsky, Ellen, Kerstin Aumann, and James T. Bond. *Times Are Changing: Gender and Generation at Work and Home.* New York: Families and Work Institute, 2011. http://familiesandwork.org/site/research/reports/Times_Are_Changing.pdf.

Game Golf. Home page. Accessed August 3, 2013. http://www.gameyourgame.com/.

Gandia, Ed. *2012 Freelance Industry Report.* Marietta, GA: International Freelancers Academy; Richland, GA: Back of the House, 2012. https://s3.amazonaws.com/ifdconference/2012report/Freelance+Industry+Report+2012+updated.pdf.

Gaydos, Mark. "Virtual Agents Will Replace Live Customer Services Reps. Pro: Clearly Destined." *Businessweek.* Accessed August 1, 2013. http://www.businessweek.com/debateroom/archives/2010/07/virtual_agents_will_replace_live_customer_service_reps.html.

Global Human Capital Gender Advisory Council. *The Leaking Pipeline: Where Are Our Female Leaders? 79 Women Share Their Stories.* London: PricewaterhouseCoopers, 2008. http://www.pwc.com/en_GX/gx/women-at-pwc/assets/leaking_pipeline.pdf.

Go Government. "Frequently Asked Questions." Accessed August 11, 2013. http://gogovernment.org/about/faqs.php.

Google. "Glass. What It Does." Accessed August 3, 2013. http://www.google.com/glass/start/what-it-does/.

———. "Work at Google." Accessed July 1, 2013. http://research.google.com/workatgoogle.html.

Gorle, Peter, and Andrew Clive. *Positive Impact of Industrial Robots on Employment.* Frankfurt, Germany: International Federation of Robotics. http://www.ifr.org/uploads/media/Update_Study_Robot_creates_Jobs_2013.pdf.

Gratton, Lynda. *The Shift: The Future of Work Is Already Here.* London: HarperCollins, 2011.

Grail Research. *Consumers of Tomorrow: Insights and Observations about Generation Z.* Cambridge, MA: Grail Research, 2011. http://www.grailresearch.com/pdf/ContenPodsPdf/Consumers_of_Tomorrow_Insights_and_Observations_About_Generation_Z.pdf.

Grant, Kelli B. "Watch Out for Wearable Tech." *MarketWatch*, April 17, 2013. http://www.marketwatch.com/story/watch-out-for-wearable-tech-2013-04-17.

Green, Miranda. "California Towns Pass Law Requiring New Buildings to Have Solar Panels." *Daily Beast,* May 10, 2013. http://www.thedailybeast.com/articles/2013/05/10/california-towns-pass-law-requiring-new-buildings-to-have-solar-panels.html.

Griswold, Daniel. "Opening the World of Export Opportunity to US Small Businesses." Statement before the Committee on Small Business, United States House of Representatives, June 19, 2008. http://www.cato.org/testimony/ct-dg-20080619.html?q=/node/885.

Guardian Life Small Business Research Institute. *Women Small Business Owners Will Create 5+ Million New Jobs by 2019, Transforming the Workplace for Millions of Americans.* New York: The Guardian Life Small Business Research Institute, 2009. http://www.smallbizdom.com/

glife11pp/groups/camp_internet/@stellent_camp_website_smallbizdom/documents/report/women-small-business-owners.pdf.

Guizzo, Erico, and Evan Ackerman, "How Rethink Robotics Built Its New Baxter Robot Worker." *IEEE Spectrum,* October 2012. http://spectrum.ieee.org/robotics/industrial-robots/rethink-robotics-baxter-robot-factory-worker.

Guta, Michael. "Underwater Robotics to Grow Nearly 7 Percent in Next 4 Years." *RobotXworld,* May 20, 2013. http://www.robotxworld.com/topics/robotics/articles/338714-underwater-robotics-grow-nearly-7-percent-next-4.htm.

Hagel, John III, John Seely Brown, and Lang Davison. "Abandon Stocks, Embrace Flows." *Harvard Business Review,* January 27, 2009. http://blogs.hbr.org/bigshift/2009/01/abandon-stocks-embrace-flows.html.

Halal, William E. "Space Tourism—Intro. SB." *TechCast,* August 3, 2013. http://www.techcast.org/BreakthroughAnalysis.aspx?ID=76.

Hale, Ethan. "Your Company Needs a Mobile Strategy Yesterday—And These Numbers Prove It." *Fast Company,* October 3, 2012. http://www.fastcompany.com/3001816/your-company-needs-mobile-strategy-yesterday-and-these-numbers-prove-it.

Hall, Kathleen. "Why More Businesses Are Nearshoring in Eastern Europe." *ComputerWeekly,* July 2011. http://www.computerweekly.com/feature/Why-more-businesses-are-nearshoring-in-Eastern-Europe.

Halpern, R. Patrick. *Workforce Issues in the Nonprofit Sector.* Kansas City, MO: American Humanics Initiative for Nonprofit Sector Careers, 2006. http://www.nassembly.org/Collaborations/PeerNetworks/documents/AmericanHumanicsWorkforceLiteratureReviewandBibliography4-26-06.pdf.

Hann, Il-Horn, Siva Viswanathan, and Byungwan Koh. *The Facebook App Economy.* College Park, MD: Robert H. Smith School of Business at the University of Maryland, 2011. http://www.rhsmith.umd.edu/news/releases/2011/091911.aspx.

Harrington, Brad, Fred Van Deusen, and Beth Humberd. *The New Dad: Caring, Committed and Conflicted.* Chestnut Hill, MA: Boston College Center for Work and Family, 2011. http://www.bc.edu/content/dam/files/centers/cwf/pdf/FH-Study-Web-2.pdf.

Harrington, Elizabeth. "Less Than 50% of U.S. Households Now Led by Married Couples, Says Census Bureau." *CNSNews.com,* April 25, 2012. http://cnsnews.com/news/article/less-50-us-households-now-led-married-couples-says-census-bureau.

Heath, Nick. "Cloud Computing: What Does It Really Mean for IT Jobs?" *TechRepublic,* August 8, 2012. http://www.techrepublic.com/blog/cio-insights/cloud-computing-what-does-it-really-mean-for-it-jobs/39749168.

Helgeson, Henry. "The Best Weapon That Merchants Have to Combat 'Showrooming.'" *Business Insider,* April 28, 2013. http://www.businessinsider.com/how-to-fight-showrooming-2013-4.

Helyar, John. "Outsourcing: A Passage out of India." *Businessweek,* March 15, 2012. http://www.businessweek.com/articles/2012-03-15/outsourcing-a-passage-out-of-india.

Herrman, John. "Android's Best Augmented Reality App Hits the iPhone." *Gizmodo,* October 14, 2009. http://gizmodo.com/5381846/androids-best-augmented-reality-app-hits-the-iphone.

Hewlett, Sylvia Ann, Maggie Jackson, Laura Sherbin, Peggy Shiller, Eytan Sosnovich, and Karen Sumberg. *Bookend Generations: Leveraging Talent and Finding Common Ground.* New York: Center for Work-Life Policy, 2009.

Hewlett, Sylvia Ann, and Lauren Leader-Chivée. *The X Factor: Tapping into the Strengths of the 33-to-46-Year-Old Generation.* New York: Center for Work-Life Policy, 2011.

Hewlett, Sylvia Ann, and Carolyn Buck Luce. "Off-Ramps and On-Ramps: Keeping Talented Women on the Road to Success." *Harvard Business Review,* March 2005. http://hbr.org/2005/03/off-ramps-and-on-ramps-keeping-talented-women-on-the-road-to-success/ar/1.

Holmes, Ryan. "5 Ways Social Media Will Change the Way You Work in 2013." *CIO Network* (blog). *Forbes,* December 11, 2012. http://www.forbes.com/sites/ciocentral/2012/12/11/5-ways-social-media-will-change-the-way-you-work-in-2013/.

———. "The Can't-Miss Social Media Trends for 2013." *Fast Company,* November 29, 2012. http://www.fastcompany.com/3003473/cant-miss-social-media-trends-2013.

Horn, John, and Darren Pleasance. "Restarting the US Small-Business Growth Engine." *McKinsey Quarterly,* November 2012. https://www.mckinseyquarterly.com/Restarting_the_US_small_business_growth_engine_3032.

Howe, Neil, and William Strauss. *Millennials Rising: The Next Great Generation.* New York: Vintage, 2000.

Hsu, Jeremy, and TechNewsDaily. "Why 3-D Printing Matters for 'Made in U.S.A.'" *Scientific American,* December 6, 2012. http://www.scientificamerican.com/article.cfm?id=why-3d-printing-matters.

Huang, Lee-Sean. "Four Lessons from the Social Innovation Hotbed of Brazil." *Co.EXIST* (blog). *Fast Company.* Accessed November 20, 2012. http://www.fastcoexist.com/1679295/4-lessons-from-the-social-innovation-hotbed-of-brazil.

IBISWorld, "Autonomous Underwater Vehicle Manufacturing in the US Industry Market Research Report Now Available from IBISWorld." News release. May 23, 2013. http://www.prweb.com/releases/2013/5/prweb10758108.htm.

IBM Institute for Business Value and IBM Strategy & Change. *Capitalizing on Complexity: Insights from the Global Chief Executive Officer Study.* Somers, NY: IBM Global Business Services, 2010. http://public.dhe.ibm.com/common/ssi/ecm/en/gbe03297usen/GBE03297USEN.PDF.

Im, Jimmy. "Will Conrad's New Concierge App Replace the Real Thing?" *HotelChatter,* December 18, 2012. http://www.hotelchatter.com/story/2012/12/17/163345/56/hotels/Will_Conrad's_New_Concierge_App_Replace_The_Real_Thing%3F.

IMCA. "Global Careers in Marine Contracting." Accessed August 5, 2013, http://www.imca-int.com/careers.aspx.

———. "Make the Move." Accessed August 5, 2013. http://www.imca-int.com/careers/make-the-move.aspx.

InnovationNewsDaily. "Robotic 'Mule,' DARPA's LS3 Model, May Aid Soldiers." *Huffington Post,* February 8, 2012. http://www.huffingtonpost.com/2012/02/08/ls3-robot-mule_n_1263726.html.

Institute for the Future for Apollo Research Institute. *The Future of Work.* Palo Alto, CA: Institute for the Future, 2012; Phoenix, AZ: Apollo Research Institute. http://apolloresearchinstitute.com/research-studies/workforce-preparedness/future-work (site discontinued).

———. *Future of Work Report: Flat-World Labor.* Palo Alto, CA: Institute for the Future, 2012; Phoenix, AZ: Apollo Research Institute. http://apolloresearchinstitute.com/sites/default/files/future-of-work-report-flat-world-labor.pdf (site discontinued).

———. *Future of Work Report: Data-Intensive Work.* Palo Alto, CA: Institute for the Future; Phoenix: Apollo Research Institute, 2012. http://apolloresearchinstitute.com/sites/default/files/future-of-work-report-data-intensive_work.pdf (site discontinued).

———. *Future of Work Report: Smart Machines.* Palo Alto, CA: Institute for the Future; Phoenix: Apollo Research Institute, 2012. http://apolloresearchinstitute.com/research-studies/workforce-preparedness/future-work-skills-2020-cognitive-load-management (site discontinued).

———. *Future of Work Report: The VUCA World.* Palo Alto, CA: Institute for the Future; Phoenix, AZ: Apollo Research Institute, 2011. http://apolloresearchinstitute.com/sites/default/files/future-of-work-report-the-vuca-world.pdf (site discontinued).

———. *Future Work Skills 2020*. Palo Alto, CA: Institute for the Future, 2011. http://www.iftf.org/uploads/media/SR-1382A_UPRI_future_work_skills_sm.pdf

Iowa Future. "Iowa, Did You Know?" *YouTube* video, 7:38. Uploaded August 4, 2011. http://www.youtube.com/watch?v=dMsNct4X_GU.

Jacek Spiewla.com. "BeatGlove." Accessed August 3, 2013. http://www.jacekspiewla.com/projects/beatglove/.

Jacobsen, Linda A., Mark Mather, and Genevieve Dupuis. *Household Change in the United States.* Washington, DC: Population Reference Bureau, 2012. http://www.prb.org/pdf12/us-household-change-2012.pdf.

James, Michael. "Working in America: Public vs. Private Sector." *ABC News*, February 18, 2011. http://abcnews.go.com/blogs/politics/2011/02/working-in-america-public-vs-private-sector/.

Jarvis, Jeff. "Newspapers in 2020." *BuzzMachine* (blog), September 6, 2007. http://buzzmachine.com/newspapers-in-2020.

Jawbone. "UP." Accessed August 3, 2013. https://jawbone.com/up.

Jeong, May. "Number of Stay-at-Home Dads on the Rise." *Economy Lab* (blog). *Globe and Mail*, June 17, 2011. http://www.theglobeandmail.com/report-on-business/economy/economy-lab/daily-mix/number-of-stay-at-home-dads-on-the-rise/article2065381/.

Jones, Sam, and Maev Kennedy. "More Than a Third of Babies Born in 2012 Will Live to 100, Report Predicts." *Guardian*, March 26, 2012. http://www.guardian.co.uk/society/2012/mar/26/third-babies-2012-live-100.

Joy, Lois, Nancy M. Carter, Harvey M. Wagner, and Sriram Narayanan. *The Bottom Line: Corporate Performance and Women's Representation on Boards*. Princeton, NJ: Catalyst, 2007. http://www.catalyst.org/file/139/bottom%20line%202.pdf.

Journalism Degree.com. "Social Media Careers." Accessed August 3, 2013. http://www.journalismdegree.com/social-media-careers/.

Juergen, Michelle. "The Top 50 Entrepreneurship Programs." *Entrepreneur*. October 2011, 2012. http://www.entrepreneur.com/article/220327.

Juniper Research. "Augmented Reality Mobile Apps to Generate Nearly $300mn in Revenues, Juniper Report Finds." News release. November 6, 2012. https://www.juniperresearch.com/press-releases.php/http:/press-releases.php?category=2.

Kamenetz, Anya. "The Four-Year Career." *Fast Company*, February 2012. http://www.fastcompany.com/1802731/four-year-career.

Kane, Tim. *The Importance of Startups in Job Creation and Job Destruction*. Kansas City, MO: Ewing Marion Kauffman Foundation, 2010. http://www.kauffman.org/uploadedfiles/firm_formation_importance_of_startups.pdf.

Kelley, Donna J., Slavica Singer, and Mike Herrington. *Global Entrepreneurship Monitor. United States Report 2011*. London: Global Entrepreneurship Research Association. 2011. http://www.gemconsortium.org/docs/2618/gem-unied-states-2011-report.

King, Steve, and Carolyn Ockels. *Intuit Future of Small Business Report. Research Brief: Defining Small Business Innovation*. Mountain View, CA: Intuit, 2009, http://http-download.intuit.com/http.intuit/CMO/intuit/futureofsmallbusiness/intuit_fosb_report_march_2009.pdf.

King, Steve, Anthony Townsend, and Carolyn Ockels. *Intuit Future of Small Business Report. Second Installment: Technology Trends and Small Business*. Palo Alto, CA: Institute for the Future for Intuit, 2007. http://http-download.intuit.com/http.intuit/CMO/intuit/futureofsmallbusiness/SR-1037B_intuit_tech_trends.pdf.

Klein, Karen E. "Are Entrepreneurs Born or Made?" *Businessweek,* July 23, 2010. http://www.businessweek.com/smallbiz/content/jul2010/sb20100723_154719.htm.

Klotz, Irene. "U.S. Space Tourism Set for Takeoff By 2014, FAA Says." *Reuters*, March 21, 2012. http://www.reuters.com/article/2012/03/21/uk-usa-space-tourism-idUSLNE82K01420120321.

Krupnick, Ellie. "Twitter Dress: Nicole Scherzinger Debuts Electronic Outfit by CuteCircuit," *Huffington Post*, November 2, 2012. http://www.huffingtonpost.com/2012/11/02/twitter-dress-nicole-scherzinger-photos_n_2064299.html.

Damon Lavrinc. "Apple, Google Just Killed Portable GPS Devices." *Wired*, June 12, 2012. http://www.wired.com/autopia/2012/06/gps-devices-are-dead/.

Li, Anita. "Meet Baxter: A Robot with Common Sense." *Mashable*, September 19, 2012. http://mashable.com/2012/09/19/baxter-robot-work/.

Libava, Joel. "Franchise Failure Rate: Myths and Facts." *American Express Open Forum*, December 9, 2008. https://www.openforum.com/articles/franchise-failure-rate-myths-and-facts-1/.

Lindsay, Greg. "HP Invests a 'Central Nervous System for Earth' and Joins the Smarter Planet Sweepstakes." *Fast Company*. Accessed August 3, 2013. http://www.fastcompany.com/1548674/hp-invents-central-nervous-system-earth-and-joins-smarter-planet-sweepstakes.

Loosvelt, Derek. "Do You Fit into Google's Culture?" *Vault*, January 25, 2012. http://blogs.vault.com/blog/resumes-cover-letters/do-you-fit-into-googles-culture/.

Lunden, Ingrid. "In Mobile Apps, Free Ain't Free, But Cambridge University Has a Plan to Fix It." *TechCrunch*, March 6, 2012. http://techcrunch.com/2012/03/06/in-mobile-apps-free-aint-free-but-cambridge-university-has-a-plan-to-fix-it/.

Madden, Mary, and Kathryn Zickhur. *65% of Online Adults Use Social Networking Sites.* Washington, DC: Pew Research Center, 2011. http://www.ucsf.edu/sites/default/files/legacy_files/PIP-SNS-Update-2011.pdf.

Mainiero, Lisa A., and Sherry E. Sullivan. "Kaleidoscope Careers: An Alternate Explanation for the 'Opt-Out' Revolution." *Academy of Management Executive* 19, no. 1 (2005): 106–23.

———. *The Opt-Out Revolt: Why People Are Leaving Companies to Create Kaleidoscope Careers.* Mountain View, CA: Davies-Black, 2006.

Maitland, Alison, and Peter Thomson. *Future Work: How Businesses Can Adapt and Thrive in the New World of Work.* Basingstoke, UK: Palgrave Macmillan, 2011.

Malkinson, Terrance. "Globalization and Your Career: Building Career Resilience." *IEEE-USA Today's Engineer Online*, February 2006. http://www.todaysengineer.org/2006/Feb/globalization.asp.

Malone, Thomas W. *The Future of Work: How the New Order of Business Will Shape Your Organization, Your Management Style, and Your Life.* Cambridge, MA: Harvard Business School Press, 2004.

Maney, Dave. "Why the Middle Market Matters—Now More Than Ever." *CNBC*, September 26, 2011. http://www.cnbc.com/id/44639661.

Mannion, James. "Top 10 Reasons to Consider a Government Job." *Netplaces*. Accessed August 11, 2013. http://www.netplaces.com/government-jobs/so-you-want-to-work-for-the-government/top-ten-reasons-to-consider-a-government-job.htm.

———. "A Wealth of Opportunities." *Netplaces*. Accessed August 8, 2012. http://www.netplaces.com/government-jobs/so-you-want-to-work-for-the-government/a-wealth-of-opportunities.htm.

Manoogian, John III. "How Free Apps Can Make More Money Than Paid Apps." *TechCrunch*, August 26, 2012. http://techcrunch.com/2012/08/26/how-free-apps-can-make-more-money-than-paid-apps/.

Manyika, James, Michael Chui, Brad Brown, Jacques Bughin, Richard Dobbs, Charles Roxburgh, and Angela Hung Byers. *Big Data: The Next Frontier for Innovation, Competition, and Productivity.* Washington, DC: McKinsey Global Institute, 2011.

Manyika, James, and Charles Roxburgh. *The Great Transformer: The Impact of the Internet on Economic Growth and Prosperity.* Washington, DC: McKinsey Global Institute, 2011. http://www.mckinsey.com/insights/mgi/research/technology_and_innovation/the_great_transformer.

Matos, Kenneth, and Ellen Galinsky. *2012 National Study of Employers*. New York: Families and Work Institute, 2012. http://familiesandwork.org/site/research/reports/NSE_2012.pdf.

Matson, Eric. "Project: You." *Fast Company*, December 31, 1997. http://www.fastcompany.com/33738/project-you.

McCue, TJ. "10 Leading Finance and Banking Apps for iPhone and iPad." *Forbes*, January 8, 2013. http://www.forbes.com/sites/tjmccue/2013/01/08/10-leading-finance-and-banking-apps-for-iphone-and-ipad/.

McKendrick, Joe. "How Cloud Computing Is Changing Many Job Descriptions." *Forbes*, December 26, 2011. http://www.forbes.com/sites/joemckendrick/2011/12/26/cloud-computing-is-changing-many-job-descriptions/.

McKinsey Global Institute. *The Social Economy: Unlocking Value and Productivity Through Social Technology. Executive Summary*. Washington, DC: McKinsey Global Institute, 2012. http://www.mckinsey.com/insights/mgi/research/technology_and_innovation/the_social_economy.

McNall, Laurel A., Aline D. Masuda, and Jessica M. Nicklin. "Flexible Work Arrangements, Job Satisfaction, and Turnover Intentions: The Mediating Role of Work-to-Family Enrichment." *The Journal of Psychology* 144 (2010): 61–81.

McNickle, Michelle. "10 Wearable Health Tech Devices to Watch." *InformationWeek*, October 31, 2012. http://www.informationweek.com/healthcare/mobile-wireless/10-wearable-health-tech-devices-to-watch/240012613.

Meinert, Dori. "Make Telecommuting Pay Off." *HR Magazine* 56 (2011).

Meister, Jeanne C., and Karie Willyerd. *The 2020 Workplace: How Innovative Companies Attract, Develop, and Keep Tomorrow's Employees Today*. New York: HarperBusiness, 2010. Kindle edition.

Merriam-Webster. "Virtual Reality." Accessed August 3, 2013. http://www.merriam-webster.com/dictionary/virtual%20reality.

Mischke, Johanna. "Wearable Technology Creates Significant Growth Opportunities." *Wearable Technologies*, August 5, 2012. http://www.wearable-technologies.com/2012/08/wearable-technology-creates-significant-growth-opportunities/.

Microsoft. "Cloud Computing to Create 14 Million New Jobs by 2015." March 5, 2012. http://www.microsoft.com/en-us/news/features/2012/mar12/03-05CloudComputingJobs.aspx.

Moretti, Enrico. *The New Geography of Jobs*. Boston: Houghton Mifflin Harcourt, 2012. Kindle edition.

Morris, Betsy, and Ruth M. Coxeter. "Executive Women Confront Midlife Crisis." *Fortune*, September 18, 1995. http://money.cnn.com/magazines/fortune/fortune_archive/1995/09/18/206085/index.htm.

Munarriz, Rick Aristotle. "5 Bricks-and-Mortar Retailers That Are Showrooming-Proof." *DailyFinance*, June 26, 2012. http://www.dailyfinance.com/2012/06/26/5-bricks-and-mortar-retailers-that-are-showrooming-proof/.

Mundy, Lisa. "Women, Money, and Power." *Time,* March 26, 2012. http://www.time.com/time/magazine/article/0,9171,2109140,00.html.

Murphy, Samantha. "Retailers Turn 'Showrooming' Into Innovation Opportunity." *Mashable,* May 19, 2013. http://mashable.com/2013/05/19/showrooming/.

New, Catherine. "Income Gap Closing: Women on Pace to Outearn Men." *Huffington Post,* March 21, 2012. http://www.huffingtonpost.com/2012/03/21/income-gap-women-make-more-men_n_1368328.html.

Nonprofit Leadership Alliance. *The Skills the Nonprofit Sector Requires of Its Managers and Leaders*. Kansas City, MO: Nonprofit Leadership Alliance, 2011. http://www.nonprofitleadershipalliance.org/cnp/cnprevalidation/Final%20Report.pdf.

North American Board of Certified Energy Practitioners. "Get Certified." Accessed August 3, 2013. http://www.nabcep.org/certification.

O'Brien, Cory. "Ray-Ban Uses Augmented Reality for Their Virtual Mirror." *The Future of Ads* (blog). Accessed August 3, 2013. http://thefutureofads.com/ray-ban-uses-augmented-reality-for-their-virtual-mirror.

O'Dell, Jolie. "Bootcamp! How Facebook Indoctrinates Every New Engineer It Hires." *VentureBeat*, March 2, 2013. http://venturebeat.com/2013/03/02/facebook-bootcamp/.

oDesk. "oDesk Announces Global Study of More Than 2,800 Businesses Indicating Significant Disruption of Traditional Hiring Model as Online Work Soars." News release. October 9, 2012. https://www.odesk.com/info/about/press/releases/odesk-announces-global-study/.

Ohio State University and General Electric Capital. *The Market That Moves America: Insights, Perspectives, and Opportunities from Middle Market Companies.* Columbus, OH: The Ohio State University; Norwalk, CT: General Electric Capital, 2011. http://www.middlemarketcenter.org/middle-market-insights-perspectives-opportunities.

O'Mara, Kelly. "Underwater Tourism: There's Nowhere to Go But Down." *Yahoo! Travel*, July 23, 2012. http://travel.yahoo.com/ideas/underwater-tourism--there-s-nowhere-to-go-but-down.html?page=all.

O'Neil, Deborah, and Diana Bilimoria. "Women's Career Development Phases: Idealism, Endurance, and Reinvention." *Career Development International* 10, no. 3 (2005): 168-89.

O'Neil, Deborah, Margaret M. Hopkins, and Diana Bilimoria. "Women's Careers at the Start of the 21st Century: Patterns and Paradoxes." *Journal of Business Ethics* 80 (2008): 727–43. doi:10.1007/s10551-007-9465-6.

O'Neill, Michael. *Future Work and Work Trends.* East Greenville, PA: Knoll Workplace Research, 2009. http://www.knoll.com/research/downloads/WP_future_work_work_trends.pdf.

Ott, Adrian. "How Social Media Has Changed the Workplace." *Fast Company*, November 11, 2012. http://www.fastcompany.com/1701850/how-social-media-has-changed-workplace-study.

Palmer, Kimberly. "The Rise of the Stay-at-Home Dad." *Alpha Consumer* (blog). *US News and World Report*, June 26, 2009. http://money.usnews.com/money/blogs/alpha-consumer/2009/06/26/the-rise-of-the-stay-at-home-dad.

Passel, Jeffrey, and D'Vera Cohn. *U.S. Population Projections: 2005–2050.* Washington, DC: Pew Research Center, 2008. http://www.pewsocialtrends.org/files/2010/10/85.pdf.

PepsiCo.com. "Real World Leadership." Accessed July 27, 2013. http://www.pepsico.com/Careers/Why-Work-at-PepsiCo/Training-and-Development.html.

Peter D. Hart Research Associates. *Encore Career Survey.* New York: MetLife Foundation/Civic Ventures, 2008. http://www.civicventures.org/publications/surveys/encore_career_survey/Encore_Survey.pdf.

Pew Research Center. "Millennials: Confident. Connected. Open to Change." February 24, 2010. http://www.pewsocialtrends.org/2010/02/24/millennials-confident-connected-open-to-change/.

———. "Modern Marriage." July 18, 2007. http://www.pewsocialtrends.org/2007/07/18/modern-marriage/.

———. *Most Middle-Aged Adults Are Rethinking Retirement Plans.* Pew Research Center: Washington, DC, 2009. http://www.pewsocialtrends.org/2009/05/28/most-middle-aged-adults-are-rethinking-retirement-plans/.

———. *The Rise of Asian Americans.* Washington, DC: Pew Research Center, 2012. http://www.pewsocialtrends.org/files/2012/06/SDT-The-Rise-of-Asian-Americans-Full-Report.pdf.

Powell, Gary N., and Lisa A. Mainiero. "Cross-Currents in the River of Time: Conceptualizing the Complexities of Women's Careers." *Journal of Management* 18, no. 2 (1992): 215–37.

Pramis, Joshua. "Number of Mobile Phones to Exceed World Population." *Digital Trends*, February 28, 2013. http://www.digitaltrends.com/mobile/mobile-phone-world-population-2014/.

PricewaterhouseCoopers. "Managing Tomorrow's People. Key Findings." Accessed January 3, 2013. http://www.pwc.com/gx/en/managing-tomorrows-people/future-of-work/key-findings.jhtml.

———. *Talent Mobility: 2020 and Beyond.* London: PricewaterhouseCoopers, 2012. http:// www.pwc.com/en_GX/gx/managing-tomorrows-people/future-of-work/pdf/pwc-talent-mobility-2020.pdf.

Quinn, Joseph F. "Work, Retirement, and the Encore Career: Elders and the Future of the American Workforce." *Generations* 34, no. 3 (2010): 45–55.

Roberts, Michael. "The Pros and Cons of a Government Job." *About.com.* Accessed August 11, 2013. http://govcareers.about.com/od/StartingOut/a/The-Pros-And-Cons-Of-A-Government-Job.

Robertson, Kathy. "How Long Do Workers Stay in Jobs?" *Sacramento Business Journal,* December 27, 2012. http://www.bizjournals.com/sacramento/news/2012/12/27/how-long-do-americans-stay-in-jobs.html?page=all.

RobotShop. "Personal and Domestic Robots." Accessed August 3, 2013. http://www.robotshop.com/personal-domestic-robots.html.

RobotWorx. "Robotics Industry Fueling Job Growth." Accessed August 3, 2013. http://www.ro-bots.com/blog/viewing/robotics-industry-fueling-job-growth.

Rohman, Jessica. "Higher Purpose, Shared Fate." *Great Place to Work,* March 6, 2013. http://www.greatplacetowork.com/publications-and-events/blogs-and-news/1648-whole-foods.

Rosati, Fabio. "A Business of One: 5 Strategies for Successful Freelancing." *CIO Network* (blog). *Forbes,* June 4, 2012. http://www.forbes.com/sites/ciocentral/2012/06/04/a-business-of-one-5-strategies-for-successful-freelancing/.

Rosin, Hanna. "The End of Men," *The Atlantic,* July/August 2010. http://www.theatlantic.com/magazine/archive/2010/07/the-end-of-men/8135/1/.

Rubin, Courtney. "How to Make a Career in Public Service." *US News and World Report,* October 28, 2010. http://www.usnews.com/news/articles/2010/10/28/how-to-make-a-career-in-public-service.

Rutherford, Mark. "BEAR Robot Roars to the Rescue." *CNET,* August 22, 2009. http://news.cnet.com/8301-13639_3-10315369-42.html.

Saenz, Aaron. "No Humans, Just Robots—Amazing Videos of the Modern Factory." *Singularity Hub,* February 11, 2010. http://singularityhub.com/2010/02/11/no-humans-just-robots-amazing-videos-of-the-modern-factory/.

Said, Carolyn. "Google's Brin Signs Up to Be Space Tourist." *San Francisco Chronicle,* June 12, 2008. http://www.sfgate.com/news/article/Google-s-Brin-signs-up-to-be-space-tourist-3210241.php.

Salamon, Julie. *Hospital: Man, Woman, Birth, Death, Infinity, Plus Red Tape, Bad Behavior, Money, God, and Diversity on Steroids.* New York: Penguin, 2008. Kindle edition.

Salamon, Lester M., S. Wojciech Sokolowski, and Stephanie L. Geller. *Nonprofit Employment Bulletin No. 39, Holding the Fort: Nonprofit Employment During a Decade of Turmoil.* Baltimore: Johns Hopkins University Center for Civil Society Studies, 2012. http://ccss.jhu.edu/wp-content/uploads/downloads/2012/01/NED_National_2012.pdf

Simms, David, and Carol Trager. *Finding Leaders for America's Nonprofits.* New York: The Bridgespan Group, 2009. http://www.bridgespan.org/WorkArea/linkit.aspx?LinkIdentifier=id&ItemID=3824.

Seattle Post-Intelligencer, "How Cloud Computing Is Changing the IT Industry." June 13, 2013. http://www.seattlepi.com/business/article/How-Cloud-Computing-is-Changing-the-IT-Industry-4263418.php.

SensoGlove. Home page. Accessed August 3, 2013. http://www.sensoglove.com/.

Shellenbarger, Sue. "Single and Off the Fast Track." *Wall Street Journal,* May 23, 2012. http://online.wsj.com/article/SB10001424052702304791704577420130278948866.html.

Silverman, Rachel Emma. "Who's the Boss? There Isn't One." *Wall Street Journal*, June 19, 2012. http://online.wsj.com/article/SB10001424052702303379204577474953586383604.html.

Sloan Work and Family Research Network. "Questions and Answers about Generation X/Generation Y: A Sloan Work & Family Research Network Fact Sheet." Retrieved January 3, 2013. http://workfamily.sas.upenn.edu/sites/workfamily.sas.upenn.edu/files/imported/pdfs/GXGY. pdf.

US Small Business Administration. "Small Business Trends." Accessed August 8, 2013. http://www. sba.gov/content/small-business-trends.

Solar Energy Industries Association. *Solar Energy Facts: Q1, 2013*. Washington, DC: Solar Energy Industries Association, 2013. http://www.seia.org/sites/default/files/Q1%202013%20 SMI%20Fact%20Sheetv3.pdf.

The Solar Foundation. *National Solar Jobs Census 2012*. Washington, DC: The Solar Foundation, 2012. http://thesolarfoundation.org/sites/thesolarfoundation.org/files/TSF%20Solar%20 Jobs%20Census%202012%20Final.pdf.

———. "State Solar Jobs." Infographic. Accessed August 3, 2012. http://thesolarfoundation.org/ solarstates#ca.

Steadman, Ian. "Big Data and the Death of the Theorist." *Wired*, January 25, 2013. http://www. wired.co.uk/news/archive/2013-01/25/big-data-end-of-theory.

Stella Artois. "Stella Artois Launches Le Bar Guide." News release. Accessed August 3, 2013. http:// www.ab-inbev.com/pdf/SA_BarGuide.pdf.

Stevenson, Seth. "Polka Dots Are In? Polka Dots It Is!" *Slate*, June 21, 2012. http://www.slate.com/ articles/arts/operations/2012/06/zara_s_fast_fashion_how_the_company_gets_new_styles_ to_stores_so_quickly_.html.

Stillman, Jessica. "Elance Predicts the Future of Online Work." *Gigaom*, March 27, 2012. http:// gigaom.com/2012/03/27/elance-predicts-the-future-of-online-work/.

———. "Elance's Impressive Growth: Good News for Its US Users?" *Gigaom*, December 7, 2011. http://gigaom.com/2011/12/07/elances-impressive-growth-good-news-for-its-us-users/.

Suttle, Rick. "Underwater Photographer Pay Scale." *Houston Chronicle*. Accessed August 5, 2013. http://work.chron.com/underwater-photographer-pay-scale-20216.html.

Taylor, Paul, and D'Vera Cohn. "A Milestone En Route to a Majority Minority Nation," Pew Research Center, November 7, 2012. http://www.pewsocialtrends.org/2012/11/07/a-milestone-en-route-to-a-majority-minority-nation/.

Paul Taylor, Cary Funk, and Peyton Craighill, *Working after Retirement: The Gap Between Expectations and Reality*. Washington, DC: Pew Research Center, 2006. http://www.pewsocialtrends. org/files/2010/10/Retirement.pdf.

Paul Taylor, et al., *The Return of the Multi-Generational Family Household* Washington, DC: Pew Research Center, 2010. http://www.pewsocialtrends.org/files/2010/10/752-multi-generational-families.pdf.

Than, Ker. "Virgin Galactic Unveils First Tourist Spaceship." *National Geographic News*, December 8, 2009. http://news.nationalgeographic.com/news/2009/12/091208-virgin-galactic-spaceship-enterprise-branson/.

Thibodeau, Patrick. "Big Data to Create 1.9M IT Jobs in U.S. by 2015, Says Gartner." *Computerworld*, October 22, 2012. http://www.computerworld.com/s/article/9232721/Big_data_to_ create_1.9M_IT_jobs_in_U.S._by_2015_says_Gartner.

Thielfoldt, Diane, and Devon Scheef. "Generation X and the Millennials: What You Need to Know about Mentoring the New Generations." *Law Practice Today*, November 2005. http://apps. americanbar.org/lpm/lpt/articles/mgt08044.html.

ThinkGeek. "Electronic Drum Machine Shirt." Accessed August 3, 2013. http://www.thinkgeek. com/product/ebb1/#tabs.

Thompson, Derek. "The Future of America Is Freelance." *The Atlantic,* September 17, 2010. http://www.theatlantic.com/business/archive/2010/09/the-future-of-america-is-freelance/63171/.

Towers Watson. *2012 Global Workforce Study. Engagement at Risk: Driving Strong Performance in a Volatile Global Environment.* New York: Towers Watson, 2012. http://www.towerswatson.com/en/Insights/IC-Types/Survey-Research-Results/2012/07/2012-Towers-Watson-Global-Workforce-Study.

———. *The New Employment Deal: How Far, How Fast and How Enduring? Insights from the 2010 Global Workforce Study.* New York: Towers Watson, 2010.

Trendwatching.com. "December 2012 Trend Briefing: 10 Crucial Consumer Trends for 2013." Accessed December 8, 2012. http://www.trendwatching.com/trends/10trends2013/.

Troianovski, Anton. "Apps: The New Corporate Cost-Cutting Tool." *Wall Street Journal,* March 5, 2013. http://online.wsj.com/article/SB10001424127887324678604578342690461080894.html.

Tulgan, Bruce. "High-Maintenance Generation Z Heads to Work." *USA Today,* June 26, 2012. http://usatoday30.usatoday.com/news/opinion/forum/story/2012-06-27/generation-z-work-millenials-social-media-graduates/55845098/1.

Underwater Welding Guide. "The Global Job Market for Underwater Welders." March 30, 2012. http://underwaterweldingguide.wordpress.com/2012/03/30/the-global-job-market-for-underwater-welders/.

US Bureau of Labor Statistics. "Charts from the American Time Use Survey." Last modified July 10, 2013. http://www.bls.gov/tus/charts/.

———. "Number of Jobs Held, Labor Market Activity, and Earnings Growth Among the Youngest Baby Boomers: Results from a Longitudinal Study." News release. July 25, 2012. http://www.bls.gov/news.release/pdf/nlsoy.pdf.

———. *Occupational Outlook Handbook, 2012–13 Edition, Career Guide to Industries.* Accessed August 3, 2013. http://www.bls.gov/ooh/About/Career-Guide-to-Industries.htm.

US Census Bureau. *2007 Economic Census: Franchise Statistics.* Washington, DC: US Census Bureau, 2007. http://www.census.gov/econ/census/pdf/franchise_flyer.pdf.

———. "Census Bureau Reports Hispanic-Owned Businesses Increase at More Than Double National Rate." News release. September 21, 2010. http://www.census.gov/newsroom/releases/archives/business_ownership/cb10-145.html.

US Department of Commerce Economics and Statistics Administration. *Women-Owned Businesses in the 21st Century.* Washington, DC: US Department of Commerce Economics and Statistics Administration, 2010. http://www.dol.gov/wb/media/Women-Owned_Businesses_in_The_21st_Century.pdf.

US Small Business Administration. *Frequently Asked Questions.* Washington, DC: US Small Business Administration, 2012. http://www.sba.gov/sites/default/files/FAQ_Sept_2012.pdf.

———. "Small Business Trends." Accessed January 25, 2012. www.sba.gov/content/small-business-trends.

———. "What Is SBA's Definition of a Small Business Concern?" Accessed February 1, 2012. http://www.sba.gov/content/what-sbas-definitionsmall-business-concern.

United States International Trade Commission. *Small and Medium-Sized Enterprises Overview of Participation in US Exports.* Investigation No. 332-508, USITC Publication 4125. January 2010. http://www.usitc.gov/publications/332/pub4125.pdf.

UPI.com. "U.S. Immigrant Population 40.4 Million." January 29, 2013. http://www.upi.com/Top_News/US/2013/01/29/US-immigrant-population-404-million/UPI-59191359490020/.

UPS.com. "Telematics." Accessed December 20, 2012. http://www.ups.com/content/us/en/bussol/browse/leadership-telematics.html.

Vizard, Michael. "Big Data and the Demise of Business Analysts." *Slashdot*, February 4, 2013. http://slashdot.org/topic/bi/big-data-and-the-demise-of-business-analysts/.

Walker, Rebecca. "Gen Y Grads More Likely to Launch Start-Ups." *USA Today*, May 8, 2010. http://usatoday30.usatoday.com/money/smallbusiness/story/2012-05-07/generation-y-entrepreneurs-small-business/54814472/1.

Washington Business Journal. "MicroStrategy Makes Mobile App to Replace Employee Photo Badge." Accessed August 3, 2013. http://www.bizjournals.com/washington/blog/techflash/2013/04/microstrategy-makes-mobile-app-to.html.

Wharton School of the University of Pennsylvania. "Declining Employee Loyalty: A Casualty of the New Workplace." *Knowledge@Wharton*, May 9, 2012. http://knowledge.wharton.upenn.edu/article.cfm?articleid=2995.

White House Project. *The White House Project: Benchmarking Women's Leadership.* Brooklyn, NY: The White House Project, 2009. http://thewhitehouseproject.org/wp-content/uploads/2012/03/benchmark_wom_leadership.pdf.

Wikipedia. "Augmented Reality." Last modified July 30, 2013. http://en.wikipedia.org/wiki/Augmented_reality.

———. "eBay." Last modified June 7, 2013. http://en.wikipedia.org/wiki/Ebay.

———. "E-learning." Last modified July 26, 2013. http://en.wikipedia.org/wiki/E_learning.

———. "Facebook." Last modified June 7, 2013. http://en.wikipedia.org/wiki/Facebook.

———. "Google." Last modified June 6, 2013. http://en.wikipedia.org/wiki/Google.

———. "Medical Robots." Last modified March 19, 2013. http://en.wikipedia.org/wiki/Medical_robots.

———. "M-learning." Last modified June 15, 2013. http://en.wikipedia.org/wiki/M-learning.

Wilen-Daugenti, Tracey .*edu: Technology and Learning Environments in Higher Education.* New York: Peter Lang, 2009.

———. *Juststaff Pulse Survey Report.* Palo Alto, CA: Juststaff, 2013. http://traceywilen.com/JustStaff_Pulse_Survey_Report.pdf.

———. *Society 3.0: How Technology Is Reshaping Education, Work and Society.* New York: Peter Lang, 2012.

Wilen-Daugenti, Tracey, Courtney L. Vien, and Caroline Molina-Ray, eds. *Women Lead: Career Perspectives from Workplace Leaders.* New York: Peter Lang, 2013.

Williams, Alex. "Just Wait Until Your Mother Gets Home." *New York Times*, August 10, 2012. http://www.nytimes.com/2012/08/12/fashion/dads-are-taking-over-as-full-time-parents.html?pagewanted=all&_r=0.

Williams, Geoff. "Reasons You Should Buy a Franchise (And Reasons You Shouldn't)." *US News and World Report*, February 27, 2013. http://money.usnews.com/money/personal-finance/articles/2013/02/27/reasons-you-should-buy-a-franchise-and-reasons-you-shouldnt.

Yates, Mick. "Big Data Kills the Pilot?" *LeaderValues* (blog), May 26, 2013. http://www.leader-values.com/wordpress/?p=6270.

Zillow. "Americans Spend More Time Researching Car Purchase Than Their Home Loan, According to Recent Zillow.com® Survey." News release. April 3, 2008. http://www.reuters.com/article/2008/04/03/idUS126258+03-Apr-2008+PRN20080403.

Zupek, Rachel. "Maximizing a Non-Profit Salary." *CNN*, May 16, 2007. http://www.cnn.com/2007/US/Careers/05/16/cb.profit/.

INDEX

Dr. Tracey Wilen (www.traceywilen.com) is a prominent thought leader on the impact of technology on society, work, and careers. A former visiting scholar at Stanford University, she has held leadership positions at Apple, HP, Cisco, and the Apollo Group. Dr. Wilen has authored 11 books, including *Women Lead: Career Perspectives from Workplace Leaders* (2013) and *Society 3.0: How Technology Is Reshaping Education, Work, and Society* (2012). She has appeared on CNN, Fox, and CBS News, and in the *Wall Street Journal*, the *Chicago Tribune*, *Forbes*, the *Los Angeles Times*, and *USA Today*. She frequently contributes to the Huffington Post, the Examiner, and the Christian Science Monitor, and weekly appears on radio shows across the US as an expert guest.

Dr. Wilen is a global speaker on the impact of technology on work, careers, and women's leadership. She was honored by the *San Francisco Business Times* as a 2012 Most Influential Woman in Bay Area Business.

Dr. Courtney L. Vien is a freelance writer and editor based in Durham, NC. A former senior editor for the Apollo Research Institute, she is the author of five books, including *Women Lead: Career Perspectives from Workplace Leaders* (2013), and numerous web and print articles, reports, and white papers. Dr. Vien has taught film, writing, and literature and holds a doctorate in English from the University of North Carolina at Chapel Hill. Her portfolio is available at www.courtneyvien.com.

Gary Daugenti is the president and founder of executive search firm Gent & Associates (www.gentinc.com). He has over 20 years' recruiting experience and over 25 years of business experience in technology and management consulting. Daugenti has personally staffed individual contributors, managers, directors, vice presidents, and C-level applicants at over 200 firms throughout the United States as well as providing executive outplacement services. His education includes a MBA in global management, recruiter training by Management Recruiters International, a certificate in computer networking, and a private pilot's license. Daugenti hails from Union County, NJ and is an alumnus of Kean University.